**THE PARIS**  **E**

# Gerald Lloyd

# The
# Parish Councillor's Guide

The law and practice of parish, town and community
councils in England and Wales

*by*

**PAUL CLAYDEN**

TWENTIETH EDITION

Shaw & Sons

Shaw's
*Since 1750*

*Published by*
Shaw & Sons Limited
Shaway House
21 Bourne Park
Bourne Road
Crayford
Kent DA1 4BZ

**www.shaws.co.uk**

© Shaw & Sons Limited 2009

First published .................................................. 1922

Twentieth Edition .......................... November 2009

ISBN 978 0 7219 0518 1

A CIP catalogue record for this book is available
from the British Library

*Printed in Great Britain by*
Bell & Bain Limited, Glasgow

# CONTENTS

# Contents

vi

# Contents

# Contents

# Contents

# Contents

## Contents

# Contents

# Contents

# Contents

## PREFACE TO THE TWENTIETH EDITION

For over 80 years *The Parish Councillor's Guide*, under a series of editors, has attempted to meet the queries of generations of parish councillors and their clerks.

Although it is less than three years since the previous edition, some important changes in the law have taken place. These include: new provisions relating to reviews of parishes in England in the Local Government and Public Involvement in Health Act 2007, with the power to create parishes in Greater London; the extension to some parish councils of the power to promote well-being enacted by the Local Government Act 2000; the removal of local councils from the ambit of the best value legislation (also in the L.G.P. I.H.A. 2007); new codes of conduct for councillors in both England and Wales; new regulations on allowances for community councillors in Wales; new election rules; revised accounting guidance and practice; and the coming into force of much of the Commons Act 2006. There have also been many detailed changes in regulations and orders made by statutory instrument.

Parish councils are some of the great survivors among our governmental institutions. They were the only councils not abolished by the Local Government Act 1972, albeit reconstituted as community councils in Wales, and have now been in existence for more than 111 years. Long may they prosper as an admirable example of the benefits to our governmental system of local decision-making by elected representatives of the people.

*Paul Clayden*

# EXPLANATION OF TERMS

Unless otherwise stated:

"parish council" means a parish council in England, a community council in Wales and a town council in either;

"parish meeting" means a parish meeting in England, a community meeting in Wales and a town meeting in either;

"parish" means a parish in England and a community in Wales;

a reference to a district or unitary council in England includes a county or county borough council in Wales;

a reference to a principal council includes a London borough council unless specifically excepted.

In England, central government has various powers in relation to parish councils. Those powers are mostly exercised by the Secretary of State for Communities and Local Government. In Wales, the powers formerly exercised by the Secretary of State for Wales have been transferred to the National Assembly for Wales. In this book, the Secretary of State means the Secretary of State in England unless otherwise stated and the National Assembly for Wales in Wales, or both, according to the context.

"C.L.G." means Communities and Local Government.

"D.E.F.R.A." means the Department for Environment, Food and Rural Affairs.

# EXPLANATION OF THE FOOTNOTES

References to Acts of Parliament, Statutory Instruments and court cases are given in the footnotes for those readers who wish to refer to relevant sources.

Acts of Parliament which have been amended or modified may be noted by the phrase "as amended". Many of the Acts are given abbreviations of title followed by the year in which they received the Royal assent.

The full titles of these Acts and other abbreviations are given below and on the next page:

| | |
|---|---|
| Art. | Article of a Statutory Instrument |
| r. | Rule of a Statutory Instrument |
| Reg. | Regulation of a Statutory Instrument |
| s. or ss. | Section or Sections of an Act |
| Sch. | Schedule to an Act or Statutory Instrument |
| S.I. | Statutory Instrument |
| A.A. 1922 | Allotments Act 1922 |
| A.A. 1925 | Allotments Act 1925 |
| A.A. 1950 | Allotments Act 1950 |
| A.C.A. 1998 | Audit Commission Act 1998 |
| A.S.B.A. 2003 | Anti-social Behaviour Act 2003 |
| C.A. 1968 | Countryside Act 1968 |
| C.A. 2006 | Commons Act 2006 |
| Ch.A. 1993 | Charities Act 1993 |
| Ch.A. 2006 | Charities Act 2006 |
| C.J.P.O.A. 1994 | Criminal Justice and Public Order Act 1994 |
| C.N.A.E.A. 2005 | Clean Neighbourhoods and Environment Act 2005 |
| C.R.O.W.A. 2000 | Countryside and Rights of Way Act 2000 |
| H.A. 1980 | Highways Act 1980 |
| H.P.A. 1986 | Housing and Planning Act 1986 |
| L.G.A. 1894 | Local Government Act 1894 |
| L.G.A. 1958 | Local Government Act 1958 |
| L.G.A. 1972 | Local Government Act 1972 |
| L.G.A. 1974 | Local Government Act 1974 |
| L.G.A. 1986 | Local Government Act 1986 |

# Explanation of the footnotes

## ABSENCE FROM MEETINGS

**(See Disqualifications for Office of Parish Councillor)**

## ACCEPTANCE OF GIFTS

**(See Property of Parish Council)**

## ACCEPTANCE OF OFFICE

**(See Parish Councillor)**

## ACCIDENTS

**(See Insurance)**

## ACCOUNTS

**(See *also* Audit—Books and Documents—Expenses and Expenditure—Inspection of Documents—Inspection of Parish Property—Value Added Tax)**

Every parish council must make arrangements for the proper administration of its financial affairs and must secure that one of its officers is responsible for the administration of those affairs.[1] He is known as the responsible financial officer (RFO). (*See also* "Treasurer".) In practice, the clerk is usually appointed as the RFO. It is the duty of the RFO to determine the form and content of the council's accounts and supporting records, subject to any directions from the council and to compliance with the Accounts and Audit Regulations 2003 (as amended) (in England) and the Accounts and Audit Regulations 2005 (in Wales).

---

[1] L.G.A. 1972, s. 151.

1

The two sets of Regulations are largely identical.[1] The RFO must ensure that the accounts and records are maintained in accordance with proper practices and kept up to date.[2]

The accounts must be made up to 31st March in each year and must be prepared in compliance with the 2003 and 2005 Regulations. They prescribe different requirements for different categories of council as follows:–

1. Councils (and parish meetings in parishes without councils) with a gross income or expenditure (whichever is the higher) for the year, and for each of the two immediately preceding years, which is less than £200,000 (£100,000 in Wales) must produce in accordance with the annual return:

   (i) a record of receipts and payments in relation to that year; or

   (ii) an income and expenditure account and statement of balances in relation to that year.

2. Councils and parish meetings with a gross income or expenditure (whichever is the higher) of £200,000 or more (£100,000 in Wales and not exceeding £1 million there), for the year and for each of the two immediately preceding years must likewise produce an income and expenditure account and a statement of balances in relation to that year.

Once the accounts have been prepared, the RFO must sign and date them and must certify that they present

---

[1] Accounts and Audit Regulations 2003 (S.I. 533); Accounts and Audit (Amendment) (England) Regulations 2006 (S.I. 564); Accounts and Audit (Wales) Regulations 2005 (S.I. 368).

[2] A.C.A. 1998, s. 2; Accounts and Audit Regulations 2003 (S.I. 533) and Accounts and Audit (Wales) Regulations 2005 (S.I. 368).

fairly the financial position of the council for the relevant accounting period. Once signed, dated and certified, the accounts must be approved by resolution of the council or of a relevant committee (e.g. a finance committee). The approval is to be given as soon as practicable after the period to which it relates and in any event within six months after the end of the period.

The approved accounts must be audited and publicised (*see* "Audit").

All cheques must be signed by two councillors.[1] It is a good practice for cheques to be signed at the meeting of the council or committee at which the relevant accounts for payment are authorised. It is also good practice for cheque counterfoils to be signed or initialled by the cheque signatory as a guard against fraud or falsification. Cheques should never be signed when blank.

As to the accounts of a charity administered by the council, *see* "Charities".

Where a council makes a grant or loan, or provides a guarantee, to a voluntary body exceeding £2,000, it must require from that body a statement setting out the way in which the money has been applied.[2] This can readily be done by the body supplying the council with a copy of its annual report and accounts.

Parish council accounts must be open to inspection by any member of the council at all reasonable times without payment. Obstruction of such inspection is punishable with a fine not exceeding level one on the standard scale (currently £200). (*See* "Inspection of documents".)

---

[1]  L.G.A. 1972, s. 151.
[2]  L.G.A. 1972, s. 137A (inserted by L.G.H.A. 1989).

# ACCUMULATION OF FUNDS

## (See Funds and Accumulations)

# ACQUISITION OF LAND

## (See Compulsory Purchase of Land—Property of Parish Council)

# ACTIONS

## (See Legal Proceedings)

# ACTS, LOCAL

## (See Bills in Parliament—Local Act Powers)

# ADMISSION OF PUBLIC TO COUNCIL MEETINGS

## (See Meetings of Parish Council)

# ADVISORY COMMITTEES

## (See Committees)

# AGENCY

## (See also Committees—Joint Committees)

There is a general power[1] for a county or district council to transfer the administration of any statutory function, except those of levying a rate, issuing a precept, borrowing money or approving a scheme for local lotteries, to a parish council by mutual agreement. Since the statutory function

---

[1] L.G.A. 1972, s. 101.

remains one which is vested in the principal council and the function itself is not transferred (only its administration or discharge), it follows that the parish council is acting as an agent for the principal council. Consequently the principal council remains responsible for the expenses involved. Indeed, the principal council can continue to exercise the function notwithstanding the arrangement, although this would be liable to cause confusion in practice.

Furthermore, a parish council exercising any function, whether directly or as an agent, may arrange for the discharge of the function by a committee, a sub-committee or an officer, but again this does not prevent the council from itself continuing to administer the function. Any committee may itself arrange for the discharge of a function by a sub-committee or officer, unless the council otherwise directs and similarly any sub-committee may arrange for the discharge of any function by an officer with the same proviso. (*See* "Committees".)

These are purely administrative arrangements and do not affect the basic responsibility of the authority upon which the function is granted by statute to ensure the proper performance of the function.

## AGENDA

**(See Meetings of Parish Council)**

## AGREEMENTS WITH OTHER PARISH COUNCILS

**(*See also* Agency—Joint Committees—Lighting— Parking Places—Roadside Seats and Shelters)**

A parish council may agree with any other parish council to discharge any of its functions jointly, and this may be done by a joint committee or by an officer of one of the councils.[1] Clearly this involves mutual agreement both with regard to the administrative arrangements and to the contributions which each authority will make to any capital or revenue expenditure.[2] In the case of joint committees only, if any dispute occurs on the apportionment of the expenses *of the committee*, this can be settled by the district council.[3]

This power may usefully be resorted to, for example, in the acquisition of a right of way in another parish or the acquisition of land for a recreation ground or swimming pool.

## AGRICULTURAL HOLDINGS

### (See Allotments)

## ALLOTMENTS

### (See *also* Compulsory Purchase of Land—Loans to Parish Council)

Parish councils have power to provide allotments for personal cultivation, and have a *duty* to do so where there is an unsatisfied demand.[4] They must on this point consider any written representations by six parliamentary electors or council tax payers resident in the parish.[5]

A parish council is not bound to provide allotments other than allotment gardens.[6] The term "allotment garden"

---

[1] L.G.A. 1972, s. 101(5).
[2] L.G.A. 1972, s. 136.
[3] L.G.A. 1972, s. 103.
[4] S.H.A.A. 1908, s. 23(1).
[5] S.H.A.A. 1908, s. 23(2).
[6] A.A. 1950, s. 9.

6

means an allotment not exceeding forty poles, i.e. 1,210 square yards, in extent which is wholly or mainly cultivated by the occupier for the production of vegetable or fruit crops for consumption by himself or his family.[1] Allotments may not be sub-let without the consent of the parish council.[2]

An allotment which is used for commercial cultivation may become an agricultural holding and thus subject to special rules as to notice to quit.

Formerly a separate account was required to be kept of allotments, and a surplus on this account could not be disposed of for other purposes without the consent of the Secretary of State. However, these requirements have now been abolished.[3] Nevertheless it remains advisable to keep a separate account in respect of allotments. Statutory allotment land, that is land purchased specifically for allotments purposes or formally appropriated for such use by a resolution of the council, must not be sold or appropriated for other purposes without the consent of the Secretary of State.[4]

Allotments are to be let at such rent as a tenant may reasonably be expected to pay, but a lower rent may be charged to a person if the council is satisfied that there exist special circumstances affecting that person which render it proper for it to let the land to him at a lower rent. Where the yearly rent exceeds £1.25, not more than a quarter's rent shall be payable in advance.[5]

Allotments are exempt from non-domestic rates.

---

[1] A.A. 1922, s. 22(1).
[2] S.H.A.A. 1908, s. 27(4).
[3] L.G.P.L.A. 1980, Sch. 5, para 2.
[4] A.A. 1925, s. 8, as amended.
[5] A.A. 1950, s. 10.

The council may make rules for regulating the letting of allotments, defining the persons eligible to be tenants, the notices to be given for lettings, the size of allotments, the conditions under which they are to be cultivated, and the rents.[1] These rules no longer require the approval of the Secretary of State.[2] The council may appoint managers, who may be wholly or partly ratepayers who are not members of the council. Such managers may do anything which the council could do in regard to allotments, including having the power to spend money. If they spend money, the expenses are deemed to be expenses of the local council.[3]

Rules make provision for reasonable notice to be given of the determination of a tenancy but if the rent for any allotment is in arrears for not less than 40 days, or if it appears to the council that not less than three months after the beginning of the tenancy the tenant has breached the rules, one month's notice to quit may be served on the tenant.[4] However, there are special statutory rules for allotments coming within the definition of an allotment garden and not attached to a cottage. The tenancy of such an allotment garden is not ordinarily to be terminable except by twelve months' notice to quit expiring on or before 6th April or on or after 29th September. Exceptions are re-entry after three months' written notice where the land is required for building, mining or other industrial purpose, for the purposes of a public undertaking or by the local authority for the purpose for which it was acquired; and re-entry for non-payment of rent or breach of any condition of the tenancy or on bankruptcy.[5]

---

[1] S.H.A.A. 1908, s. 28.
[2] L.G.P.L.A. 1980, Sch. 5, para 1.
[3] S.H.A.A. 1908, s. 29.
[4] S.H.A.A. 1908, s. 30.
[5] A.A. 1922, s. 1, and A.A. 1950, s. 1.

In respect of an allotment garden not attached to a cottage, compensation for growing crops and manure is payable by the council if the tenancy is terminated by notice to quit, or by re-entry for any of the above-mentioned purposes after three months' notice. If the tenancy is terminated between 29th September and 11th October inclusive, the tenant has three weeks in which to remove the crops.[1]

In addition, where the tenancy is terminated by re-entry for any of the purposes mentioned above, compensation for disturbance, in amount equal to one year's rent, is payable by the council.[2]

Where the parish council is itself a tenant, it may recover compensation from the head lessor in similar circumstances to those outlined in the foregoing two paragraphs.[3]

Where the tenant of an allotment garden not attached to a cottage quits the land on the termination of the tenancy, the council may recover compensation from the tenant equal to the cost of making good any deterioration of the land caused by the failure of the tenant to maintain it clean and in a good state of cultivation and fertility.

In respect of all other allotments, compensation is payable on termination of the tenancy for whatever cause. The compensation is for growing crops and manuring, and for fruit trees or bushes, drains, outbuildings, pigsties, fowlhouses or other structural improvements provided by the tenant with the previous consent in writing of the council. Compensation is determinable, in default of agreement, by a valuer appointed by the judge of the county

[1]  A.A. 1922, s. 2.
[2]  A.A. 1950, s. 3(1).
[3]  A.A. 1922, s. 2(6).

court.[1] Before the termination of his tenancy a tenant may remove any fruit trees or bushes or any erection, fencing or other improvement provided by him for which he has no claim to compensation, making good any injury caused by the removal.[2]

A parish council may let allotments to persons working on a co-operative basis.[3] If the council is of the opinion that the facilities from a society on a co-operative basis are inadequate, it may purchase fruit trees, seeds, plants, fertilisers or implements required for the purposes of allotments cultivated as gardens, whether provided by the council or otherwise, and sell any such articles to the cultivators or, in the case of implements, allow their use at a charge sufficient to cover the cost.

A parish council must be watchful that allotments are not used for purposes other than cultivation, and if necessary take steps to have any buildings, e.g. garages, removed.

If a council wishes to increase rents, it may do so at any time by agreement with the tenant. However, if the council is *imposing* an increase it must remember that it cannot do so within the period necessary for a notice to quit. It should therefore serve a formal notice to quit for the proper period on the tenant together with an offer of a new tenancy at the new rent immediately after that period, which the tenant should be asked to accept in writing. An accompanying letter can explain that the notice to quit is a formality to enable the rents to be increased.

Advice should be taken on problems arising in respect of allotments which were originally provided under Inclosure

---

[1] A.A. 1922, s. 3.
[2] S.H.A.A. 1908, s. 47.
[3] S.H.A.A. 1908, s. 27(6).

Acts or awards, e.g. fuel allotments, or under the Poor Law.

For provisions as to compulsory purchase or compulsory hiring of land for allotments, *see* "Compulsory Purchase of Land".

Most of the powers of a parish council are concurrent with those of the district council. The provision of allotments is, however, an exception. A district council in England has no direct power to provide allotments in a parish.[1] However, in Wales a county or county borough council has a concurrent power with a community council.

## ALLOWANCES TO PARISH COUNCILLORS

**(*See also* Chairman of Parish Council (for chairman's allowance))**

### England

A parish council in England may pay a basic parish allowance to its members. This is separate from the allowance payable to the chairman of the council.[2] The following considerations apply:

1. The amount of the allowance must be the same for every councillor, except that the chairman may receive a higher allowance.

2. The allowance is not payable to appointed or co-opted councillors.

---

[1] L.G.A. 1972, Sch. 29, para. 9(1).
[2] Local Authorities (Members' Allowances) (England) Regulations 2003 (S.I. 1021).

3. The allowance is annual and is not linked to any expense incurred by a councillor.

4. A councillor may choose not to receive the allowance.

5. In setting the level of the allowance, the council must have regard to the recommendations of the district council's parish remuneration panel.

6. The allowance is treated as income from an office (that of councillor) and is in principle subject to income tax under the PAYE (pay as you earn) system.

7. The allowance may be withheld for any period during which the councillor is suspended or partially suspended from office (*see* "Code of Conduct").

Travel and subsistence allowances (including travel by bicycle and other non-motorised forms of transport) may also be paid to councillors (including appointed and co-opted councillors)[1] when they carry out certain "approved duties" (*see below*) whether inside or outside the parish. Again, these allowances may be withheld for any period during which the councillor is suspended or partially suspended from office (*see* "Code of Conduct").

"Approved duty" generally means, in effect, the doing of anything approved by the parish council, or anything of a class so approved, for the purpose of, or in connection with, the discharge of the functions of the parish council or of any of its committees or sub-committees.[2]

---

[1] The maximum amount of the allowances is not prescribed, but in setting them the council should have regard to the recommendations of the parish remuneration panel.

[2] Local Authorities (Members' Allowances) (England) Regulations 2003 (S.I. 1021), Reg. 26.

## Wales

Payments may be made for expenses necessarily incurred in the performance of "approved duties" (*see above*) as follows:

(a) travelling expenses outside the community;[1]

(b) subsistence expenses outside the community;[2]

(c) attendance allowance,[3] for councillors only (i.e. not for co-opted members of committees), as payment for the performance of an "approved duty" (*see above*), being a payment of such reasonable amount as the council itself determines, subject to a ceiling in the form of an amount prescribed by the National Assembly in regulations.[4] The amount of the allowance may vary as to the time of day and the duration of the duty, but it must be the same for all members of the council entitled to the allowance in respect of a duty at the same time and of the same duration. The attendance allowance, being payable as of right, is taxable, and therefore must be declared to H.M. Revenue and Customs as income under Schedule E. In the case of members of committees who are not entitled to attendance allowance, not being councillors of that authority, there is, in substitution for the attendance allowance, a financial loss allowance, where for the purpose of performing an "approved duty" the member has necessarily suffered a loss of earnings which he would otherwise have made, or incurred additional expense (other than expense on travelling or subsistence, dealt

---

[1]  L.G.A. 1972, s. 174.
[2]  *ibid.*
[3]  L.G.A. 1972, ss. 173 and 175.
[4]  Local Authorities (Allowances for Members of Community Councils) (Wales) Regulations 2003 (S.I. 895).

with above) to which he would not otherwise have been subject. The amount of the allowance must not exceed the actual loss, or the maximum laid down by the National Assembly in regulations,[1] whichever is the less. Financial loss allowance is not taxable.

A councillor is entitled to opt for a financial loss allowance instead of receiving an attendance allowance. To do so, he must give to the council a notice in writing (a financial loss allowance notice) either within one month of his election, in which case it will apply from his election, or if not within that period then at any time thereafter, in which case it will operate after one month from the date of the notice.[2]

A community council may defray any travelling or other expenses of any member making an official or courtesy visit *on behalf of the council*, either at home or abroad. Unless the visit is abroad, the amount of any travelling or subsistence payments is subject to the limitations mentioned above.

A community council may also pay for the expense of receiving, entertaining and informing distinguished visitors to the parish, and of persons representative of or connected with local government or public service in or outside the United Kingdom.

## ALTERATION OF AREAS

### (*See also* Grouping of Parishes—Name of Parish)

### England

The Local Government Act 1992 established a system for reviewing local government areas and altering boundaries.

---

[1] Local Authorities (Allowances for Members of Community Councils) (Wales) Regulations 2003 (S.I. 895).

[2] L.G.A. 1972, s. 173A.

Under that Act, a number of unitary authorities were established which combine the functions of district and county councils. Some of these authorities are district councils to which the functions of the county council have been transferred and some are county councils to which the functions of the district council have been transferred. These provisions in the Local Government Act 1992 have been largely replaced by Part 1 of the Local Government and Public Involvement in Health Act 2007, but with the similar purpose of enabling unitary authorities to be created.

In this book unitary authorities are referred to as "unitary councils".

For parishes, Part 4 of the Local Government and Public Involvement in Health Act 2007 provides the statutory framework for reviewing areas and electoral arrangements. Such reviews are called "community governance reviews". Reviews of parish arrangements are the responsibility of principal councils (i.e. district, unitary and London borough councils). The inclusion of London borough councils means that parishes may now be established in Greater London. A review may cover the whole or part of the principal council area and may make changes in parish boundaries (including the creation, alteration or abolition of a parish) and consequential changes in electoral arrangements. As a general rule, the Secretary of State is not involved in the process of community government review and does not have to approve any changes made thereby.

The Local Government and Rating Act 1997 introduced a new procedure for creating parishes in unparished or partly unparished areas by way of petition. This procedure has been retained, with modifications, in relation to community governance reviews. A petition to hold a community governance review may be presented to the principal council, requesting the carrying out of a review for a defined area. The petition can ask for the creation of a new parish or a modification of an existing parish. The petition must be signed by at least 50% of the local government electors if the petition area has fewer than 500 electors, by at least 250 electors where the electorate is between 500 and 2,500 and by at least 10% of the electors where the electorate exceeds 2,500. The receiving principal council must respond to the petition by undertaking a review, or incorporating the terms of the petition in a review which the council is already carrying out (if any), or by rejecting the petition if one has been considered by the council within the previous two years.

Guidance on community governance reviews is contained in Communities and Local Government's publication *Guidance on Community Governance Reviews*.

### Wales

The Local Government (Wales) Act 1994 abolished the district and county councils and created new, single-tier, principal councils, called county councils or county borough councils, combining the functions of the abolished authorities. Community councils were largely unaffected by these changes.

The Local Government Boundary Commission for Wales is primarily responsible for reviewing principal local government areas and electoral arrangements in Wales. The county and county borough councils are responsible for reviewing community areas and electoral arrangements.

The whole of Wales is divided into communities (not all of them with councils). There is thus no need for a mechanism to enable new communities to be created where none exist.

For the creation and dissolution of community councils, *see* "Parish Council – Creation of parish or community council *and* Dissolution of parish or community council".

### Accretions

Every accretion from the sea, whether natural or artificial, and any part of the seashore to the low water mark, is for all purposes of local government annexed to and incorporated with the parish or parishes which such accretion or part of the seashore adjoins.[1]

## ALTERNATIVE STYLES

### (See Name and Style of Parish)

## ANNUAL MEETING OF PARISH COUNCIL

### (See *also* Meetings of Parish Council)

The parish council must, in every year, hold an annual meeting.[2] In a year involving the election of parish councillors the annual meeting must take place on the fourth day after the date of the election or within 14 days thereafter. In other years it may be held on any day in May as determined by the parish council itself.[3] The annual meeting may be held at such time as the parish council decides, but if no hour is fixed it must begin at 6 p.m. in the evening.

---

[1] L.G.A. 1972, s. 72.
[2] L.G.A. 1972, Sch. 12, para. 7(1) and 23(1).
[3] *ibid.*, para. 7(2) and 23(2).

In addition, parish councils in England must hold at least three other meetings in the course of the year.[1] Community councils in Wales may hold such other meetings as they think fit.[2]

The first business at the annual meeting is the election of a chairman.[3] (*See* "Chairman of Parish Council".) There may also be elected a vice-chairman.

If the annual meeting is the first meeting after an election, the newly elected councillors should, if they have not done so before, make at that meeting in the presence of a councillor or the clerk, and deliver to the council, a declaration of acceptance of office in the prescribed form.[4] (*See* "Parish Councillor".)

The above arrangements and those set out in the note on "Meetings of Parish Council" are the principal statutory requirements in respect of the annual meeting. Other questions of procedure may be provided for in standing orders (*see* "Standing Orders") and otherwise are for determination by the chairman at the meeting.

For annual meeting of parish meetings, *see* "Parish Meeting".

## ANTI-SOCIAL BEHAVIOUR

### (See Graffiti and Flyposting—Litter)

## APPROPRIATION OF LAND

### (See Property of Parish Council)

---

[1] L.G.A. 1972, Sch. 12, para. 8.
[2] *ibid.*, para. 24.
[3] L.G.A. 1972, ss. 15 and 34.
[4] L.G.A. 1972, s. 83.

# APPROVED DUTY

**(See Allowances to Parish Councillors)**

# ARCHIVES

**(See Books and Documents)**

# ARMISTICE DAY WREATHS

**(See Free Resource)**

# ART GALLERIES

**(See Museums and Art Galleries)**

# ARTS, THE

**(See Entertainment and the Arts)**

# AUDIT

**(See *also* Inspection of Documents—Joint Committees)**

The accounts of the parish council are audited once in every year as soon as may be after 31st March by an auditor appointed by the Audit Commission (in Wales, the Auditor General for Wales). The auditor will either be a member of the Commission's or Auditor General's staff or a private professional firm.[1]

The duty of the auditor is to see that the accounts have been prepared in accordance with legal requirements

---

[1] A.C.A. 1998, s. 3; P.A.W.A. 2004, s. 20.

and to see that proper accounting practices have been observed in the compilation of the accounts. In addition, he has a duty to consider whether, in the public interest, he should make a report on any matter arising out of, or in connection with, the accounts, in order that the matter should be considered by the council or brought to public attention.[1] If he makes such a report, he must send a copy to the Audit Commission[2] and there is a right of public inspection.[3]

An auditor has no power himself to judge whether the council has, or has not, acted within its powers. The former powers of an auditor of disallowance and surcharge have gone. If an auditor considers that any item of account is contrary to law, he may apply to the court for a declaration to that effect.[4] In addition to a declaration, the court may order rectification of the accounts.

No councillor, officer or any person acting under the council's direction has any personal liability in respect of anything done *in good faith* for the purpose of any of the council's statutory functions.[5]

An auditor may issue an advisory notice to a parish council or to an officer of the council if he has reason to believe that a decision is about to be taken, or has been taken—(a) involving unlawful expenditure, (b) to adopt a course of action which would, if concluded, result in a loss or deficiency, or (c) to enter an item of account which is unlawful. The effect of an advisory notice is that the council or its officer must give the auditor notice (not exceeding

---

[1]   A.C.A. 1998, s. 8; P.A.W.A. 2004, s. 22.
[2]   A.C.A. 1998, s. 10; P.A.W.A. 2004, s. 22.
[3]   A.C.A. 1998, s. 15; P.A.W.A. 2004, s. 30.
[4]   A.C.A. 1998, s. 17(1); P.A.W.A. 2004, s. 32.
[5]   L.G.(M.P.)A. 1976, s. 39.

21 days) if it or he intends to pursue the course of action specified in the notice.[1] In effect, therefore, an advisory notice is a formal warning and should not be ignored.

The following notes relate the usual procedure where an auditor is appointed.

The responsible financial officer arranges with the auditor the date for the commencement of the audit. He must then give at least 14 days' public notice[2] of the commencement of a period of 15 full working days during which the accounts and documents relating thereto will be available for public inspection. The notice must specify the place at which, and the hours during which, the accounts and other documents may be inspected, and also include the name and address of the auditor and the rights of local government electors in respect of the audit. The public notice may be given by advertisement (in which case the auditor must be immediately advised of the name and date of publication of the newspaper, together with a copy of the notice) or by a notice in a conspicuous place in the parish (in which case the auditor must be immediately sent a certificate to that effect). The accounts and other documents must then be made available for inspection in accordance with the notice, and copies or extracts may be taken without charge. Where there are no accounts to be audited, the chairman or clerk should certify accordingly to the auditor.

If the auditor decides to make a report on some matter, he must send a copy to the council and the Commission or Auditor General not later than 14 days after the completion of the audit. The council must then convene as soon as possible to consider the report. Not later than 14

---

[1]   A.C.A 1998, ss. 19A-19C; P.A.W.A. 2004, ss. 33-36.
[2]   Copies of this form are available from Shaw & Sons Ltd.

days after that consideration, the council must give public notice that the report is available for inspection, and allow for the taking of a copy thereof or an extract therefrom without payment.[1] Copies are to be *delivered* to any local government elector who so requests, on payment of a reasonable sum for each copy.

Any local government elector for the parish is entitled to request the auditor to provide him with an opportunity to put questions to the auditor.[2] The elector is entitled to be present at the audit, or he may be represented at the audit and may make objection to the accounts at the audit.[3]

The auditor, on the application of any person aggrieved by his decision on any matter with respect to which that person has made an objection, or of any person aggrieved by a certification by the district auditor that a sum is due from him, must state in writing the reasons for his decision, within six weeks (in Wales, 14 days) of notification.[4]

Any person aggrieved by a decision of the district auditor on any matter with respect to which he made an objection at the audit may appeal to a court of law.[5] The court, on such an appeal, may confirm, vary, or quash the auditor's decision.

The Audit Commission or Auditor General may at any time, either at the request of an elector or a council or on its own initiative, direct an auditor to hold an extraordinary audit of any of the accounts of a parish council. Also the

---

[1] A.C.A. 1998, s. 14(1); P.A.W.A. 2004, s. 29.
[2] A.C.A. 1998, s. 15(2); P.A.W.A. 2004, s. 30(2).
[3] A.C.A. 1998, s. 16(1); P.A.W.A. 2004, s. 31(1).
[4] A.C.A. 1998, s. 17(4); P.A.W.A. 2004, s. 30(6).
[5] A.C.A. 1998, s. 17(5); P.A.W.A. 2004, s. 30(7).

Secretary of State or National Assembly may direct the Commission or Auditor General to do this.[1]

Fees for audits are prescribed by the Audit Commission and the Auditor General, which have power to alter the prescribed fee in any case where the work done is less or more than that envisaged by the scale. At present parish councils are charged at an hourly rate.

The Audit Commission and the Auditor General may give directions to certain local authorities requiring them to publish information as to their performance. The Secretary of State and the National Assembly may by order bring parish and community councils respectively within the ambit of that power.[2]

## BANKRUPTCY

**(See Disqualifications for Office of Parish Councillor)**

## BATHS, WASH-HOUSES, SWIMMING POOLS AND BATHING PLACES

**(See *also* By-laws—Life-Saving Apparatus—Recreation)**

A parish council may, either within or without the parish, provide public baths and wash-houses, open or covered, and with or without drying grounds;[3] and public swimming pools and bathing places, open or covered.[4] The power to provide wash-houses includes the power to provide launderettes. The power to provide buildings or other premises includes

---

[1] A.C.A. 1998, s. 25(1) and (2); P.A.W.A. 2004, s. 30(1) and (2).
[2] A.C.A. 1998, s. 47; P.A.W.A. 2004, s. 46.
[3] P.H.A. 1936, s. 221(a).
[4] L.G.(M.P.)A. 1976, s. 19.

23

the power to equip them with such furniture, apparatus and instruments as may be necessary.[1]

With the consent of the Secretary of State loans may be raised for new provision or for the reconstruction of existing provision. (*See* "Loans to Parish Council".)

If necessary, a parish council requiring land for this service may obtain compulsory powers by an order of the district council confirmed by the Secretary of State. (*See* "Compulsory Purchase of Land".)

The council may make such charges for the use of, or admission to, any baths or wash-houses under its management as it thinks fit.[2] Notice of intention to consider a table of charges and naming a place where a copy may be inspected, must be advertised in a local newspaper at least a month before fixing any charges. Facilities at swimming pools or bathing places may be provided free or for such charge as the council considers appropriate.[3]

The council may make by-laws (subject to confirmation by the Secretary of State) for the regulation of any baths, wash-houses, swimming pools, etc. under its management, and for the regulation of persons resorting thereto, including the exclusion of undesirable persons.[4] (*See* "By-laws".)

Between 1st October and the last day of April, a parish council may close any swimming pool or bathing place under its management and use or let it for such purposes as it thinks fit and it may adapt it for those purposes.[5] The parish council may also close it temporarily at any time

---

[1] L.G.A. 1972, s. 111.
[2] P.H.A. 1936, s. 222.
[3] L.G.(M.P.)A. 1976, s. 19.
[4] P.H.A. 1936, s. 223.
[5] P.H.A. 1936, s. 226.

in order to grant exclusive use to a school or club for swimming purposes.[1]

The council may provide, lay down and maintain pipes and apparatus for conducting water to or from any baths, wash-houses, swimming pools or bathing places under its management, or which it proposes to provide, subject to certain restrictions relating to the breaking open of streets.[2]

Trustees of any public baths, wash-houses, etc. are empowered, with the consent of the committee of management (if any), to sell or lease the baths, wash-houses, etc. to a parish council.[3]

The district council may likewise provide baths, wash-houses, swimming pools and bathing places under these provisions. The parish council, instead of making provision itself, may contribute towards the expenses of another local authority or of a voluntary organisation in making such provision. Similarly, another local authority may contribute to expenses for this purpose of the parish council.[4]

Water, gas or electricity undertakers may supply water, gas or electricity to any public baths, wash-houses, etc., either without charge or on such other favourable terms as they think fit.[5]

## BENEFIT OF THE AREA

### (See Free Resource)

---

[1] P.H.A. 1936, s. 225.
[2] P.H.A. 1936, s. 227.
[3] P.H.A. 1936, s. 228.
[4] L.G.(M.P.)A. 1976, s. 19.
[5] P.H.A. 1936, s. 229.

## BEST VALUE

The Local Government and Public Involvement in Health Act 2007 removed parish councils from the ambit of the best value regime with effect from 1st April 2008.

## BICYCLE PARKS

### *(See Parking Places)*

## BILLS IN PARLIAMENT

### *(See also Local Act Powers)*

A parish council does not have the power, so important to other local authorities, of from time to time promoting a Bill in Parliament. However, a parish council has a general power to oppose any local or personal Bill in Parliament.[1]

Powers may be conferred on parish councils by local Acts promoted by other local authorities, e.g. county councils. A parish council may press its county council to include desired powers in its next local Bill. In so far as powers under local Acts in force on 1st April 1974 have not been preserved by general or local legislation or by local orders since the 1st April 1974, they expired in metropolitan counties at the end of 1979 and elsewhere at the end of 1984.[2] This does not, however, apply to local Acts passed after 1st April 1974.

## BOATING POOLS AND LAKES

### *(See Recreation)*

---

[1] L.G.A. 1972, s. 239.
[2] L.G.A. 1972, s. 262.

# BOOKS AND DOCUMENTS

## Custody

The parish council may give directions as to the custody of all public books, writings, and papers of the parish,[1] excepting the registers of baptisms, marriages, and burials, and other books and documents containing entries wholly or partly relating to the affairs of the church or to ecclesiastical charities. The expression "affairs of the church" includes the distribution of offertories or other collections made in any church.

The incumbent and churchwardens on the one hand and the parish council on the other, shall have reasonable access to all such books, documents, writings and papers in the possession of the other. Any difference as to their custody or such access shall be determined by the county council.

It is the duty of the county council (in Wales, the county or county borough council), from time to time, to inquire into the manner in which the public books and documents under the control of the parish council are kept. That council may make orders for their preservation and these orders must be complied with by the parish council.[2]

Any local government elector of the parish may, without payment, inspect the minutes of the parish council at all reasonable hours and make a copy thereof.[3] He may inspect, also without payment, and make a copy of any order or the payment of money made by the council. The accounts of the council and of the treasurer shall be open to the inspection of any member of the council and

---

[1] L.G.A. 1972, s. 226.
[2] L.G.A. 1972, s. 226(5).
[3] L.G.A. 1972, s. 228.

any such member may make a copy thereof. (As to the deposit of books and accounts, etc. prior to audit and their availability for inspection by any person interested, *see* "Audit".) (*See also* "Inspection of Documents".)

## Deposit

Various documents are required by statute or by standing orders of Parliament to be deposited with the proper officer, i.e. the clerk of the parish council; for example maps, plans, and sections of proposed works.[1] If there is no clerk, the documents must be deposited with the chairman of the council. Subject to any enactment to the contrary, a person interested in any such document may inspect the same, and take a copy thereof, on payment of 10p for the inspection, and a further sum of 10p for every hour the inspection continues beyond the first hour.[2]

In general terms, any requirement that a parish council shall keep a document of any description is satisfied if it keeps a photographic copy of the document.[3]

## Depository

The parish council is required to provide proper depositories for all the documents, books and papers belonging to the parish or community for which no provision is otherwise made; or, if the local council so requests, the district council must provide such depositories.[4] In practice many local councils have deposited their documents – other than those still required for current work – with the County Record Office. In many cases this will be the best way of ensuring the preservation of records which may ultimately be of value for local history.

---

[1]  L.G.A. 1972, s. 225.
[2]  L.G.A. 1972, s. 228(5).
[3]  L.G.A. 1972, s. 229.
[4]  L.G.A. 1972, s. 227.

## Destruction

Books, papers and documents of permanent value, such as minute books, ledgers, income registers, staff records; and all contracts, briefs and other important papers, relating to the sale and purchase of land and actions or proceedings affecting lands, should not be destroyed.

Treasurer's books; cash books and petty cash books; wages and salaries books; receipts, invoices and cheques; VAT records; contracts for works, except where there are special reasons for preservation; financial statements and loan statements; stock and store-books and rental books may be destroyed when over six years old.

Counterfoil books; order check books; agenda books; postage books; pay cards and time sheets; tenders for goods, etc. may be destroyed on the expiration of 12 months from the completion of the audit of the last entry contained in the records.

Election papers may be destroyed on the expiration of the statutory period of six months after the election.

The above list is, of course, not exhaustive. Obsolete forms, out-of-date law books, year books, periodical journals of no permanent interest, and other such miscellaneous papers may be destroyed. The County Record Office will be able to advise in cases of doubt what records are worth retaining as of future historical interest.

## Publication

Some parish councils have records of great historical interest. The Local Government (Records) Act 1962 gives parish councils wide powers to publish such records, hold exhibitions of them, and generally make them available for study by local historians and others.

As to signing and sealing documents, see "Parish Council".

## BORROWING POWERS OF PARISH COUNCIL

**(See Loans to Parish Council)**

## BOUNDARY CHANGES

**(See Alteration of Areas)**

## BRIDLEWAYS

**(See Footpaths—Highways)**

## BUILDINGS

**(See Property of Parish Council)**

## BURIAL AND CREMATION

**(*See also* Closed Churchyards—Expenses—Joint Committees—Loans to Parish Council—Mortuaries and Post-Mortem Rooms—Open Spaces)**

A parish council (and an English parish meeting where there is no parish council) is a burial authority.[1] As such a parish council may provide, or contribute towards the provision of, a cemetery or crematorium. Land may be purchased by agreement or compulsorily.[2] Burial boards,

---

[1] L.G.A. 1972, s. 214.
[2] L.G.A. 1972, s. 125 (as substituted by H.P.A. 1986, s. 43) and Sch. 26, paras. 7-9. For compulsory purchase procedure see "Compulsory Purchase of Land".

joint burial boards and joint burial committees as existing on 31st March 1974, ceased to exist on that date. However, if two or more burial authorities were involved they were obliged to set up a new joint board[1] or a joint committee.[2] (*See* "Joint Committees".)

Parish councils operate under the code based on an order made by the Secretary of State under the Local Government Act 1972. This is the Local Authorities' Cemeteries Order 1977, as amended by the Local Authorities' Cemeteries (Amendment) Order 1986.[3] Grounds hitherto maintained as burial grounds are now held as cemeteries.

The location of a cemetery very much affects the services and amenities of a local area. Thus at an early stage in the formulation of a scheme, the parish council should consult the planning authority. (*See* "Planning Permission".) The advertisement procedure in the Town and Country Planning Act 1990 applies to applications for planning permission to use land as a cemetery.

The powers of the parish council as burial authority include the provision of a crematorium.[4] A number of parish councils may combine for this purpose. The Secretary of State must first approve the plans and site and before use the council must certify to the Home Secretary that the building has been properly completed and equipped.[5] Regulations controlling cremation have been made by the Home Secretary under the Cremation Acts 1902 and 1952. More people are now cremated than buried every year in Britain.

---

[1] Under P.H.A. 1936, s. 6.
[2] L.G.A. 1972, Sch. 26, paras. 2 and 3.
[3] 1977, S.I. 204 and 1986, S.I. 1782.
[4] Cremation Act 1902, s. 4.
[5] Cremation Act 1952, s. 1 as amended by L.G.P.L.A. 1980, s. 188.

A chapel may be erected on the cemetery at the expense of the parish council,[1] and the council may lay out and embellish the grounds of the cemetery as it thinks fit.[2]

The parish council may, if it thinks fit, apply to the bishop for consecration of a cemetery.[3] A fee is payable. Only part of the ground should be consecrated.

The parish council determines the fees to be charged.[4] A table of fees must be kept, and be available for public inspection. Non-parishioners have no right of burial but are usually allowed burial on payment of a higher scale of fees. The fees payable to ministers of religion or sextons may be fixed by the burial authority. An exclusive right of burial can no longer be sold in perpetuity, but only for a fixed period not exceeding 100 years, subject to extension for up to 100 years from the date on which the extension is granted.[5] Such a right may be granted under the signature of the clerk of the council. No seal is necessary.[6]

A burial authority must keep the cemetery in good order and repair and may remove tombstones and kerbs after giving proper notice if there are no objections.[7] Vandalism in cemeteries is an offence.[8]

The keeping of a register of burials is an essential

---

[1] Local Authorities' Cemeteries Order 1977, Art. 6 (which also provides for denominational chapels to be provided by the parish council at the expense of the denomination).

[2] *ibid.*, Art. 4.

[3] *ibid.*, Art. 5.

[4] *ibid.*, Art. 15.

[5] *ibid.*, Art. 10. (The Order provides a procedure for determining rights already granted for a period greater than 75 years but unexercised for 75 years from the date of the grant.)

[6] *ibid.*, Sch. 2.

[7] *ibid.*, Arts. 4, 16 and Sch. 3.

[8] *ibid.*, Arts. 18 and 19.

requirement and so too is the keeping of a plan and register of purchased graves.[1]

Parish councils may contribute towards the expenses incurred by any other person in maintaining any place of interment in which the remains of inhabitants of the parish or community are or may be interred irrespective of the denomination of the owners.[2]

A council may, by agreement with any person, maintain any private grave or memorial for a period not exceeding 100 years.[3]

## BUS SERVICES, SUPPORT OF

### (See Transport)

## BUS SHELTERS

### (*See also* Roadside Seats and Shelters)

Local authorities, including parish councils, may provide and maintain shelters or other accommodation (e.g. seats at bus stops) for passengers by bus, coach, trolleybus or tram at stopping-places in highways within their districts or on any land abutting on such highways.[4] They may make agreements with other local authorities or transport operators for the provision and maintenance of such shelters or other accommodation, and such agreements may provide for contributions by such other local authorities or operators towards the cost of such provision and maintenance.[5]

---

[1]  Local Authorities' Cemeteries Order 1977, Arts. 9 and 11.
[2]  L.G.A. 1972, s. 214(6).
[3]  Local Authorities' Cemeteries Order 1977, Art. 10.
[4]  L.G.(M.P.)A. 1953, s. 4(1).
[5]  L.G.(M.P.)A. 1953, s. 4(2).

Either of the local authorities referred to above may be a parish council, so that the effect is to empower parish councils either to provide bus shelters themselves or to contribute towards the cost of shelters provided by other local authorities.

Where a shelter is to be erected on land abutting on a highway and the land is not already in the possession of the council, it will be necessary either to acquire the land or to obtain from the owner of the land the right to erect the shelter thereon. (*See* "Property of Parish Council" and "Compulsory Purchase of Land".)

The power to provide a shelter is subject to various consents.[1] The consent of the highway authority is required or that of railway or certain other transport undertakers in the case of certain highways repairable by those undertakers. Where the shelter is to be situated on, or on the approaches to, a bridge, the consent of the authority or other person in whom the bridge is vested is necessary. Where the shelter is to be situated on, or on the approaches to, a bridge carrying a highway over a railway, canal or inland navigation, or under a bridge carrying any of the foregoing over a highway, the consent of the undertakers concerned is necessary. In addition, where the shelter is to be situated so as to obstruct or interfere with any existing access to any land or premises abutting on the highway, the consent of the owner of the land or premises is required.

Any of these consents is not to be unreasonably withheld but may be given subject to reasonable conditions, which may include a condition that the council shall subsequently remove the shelter if reasonably required to do so. Any

---

[1]  L.G.(M.P.)A. 1953, s. 5, as amended by L.G.P.L.A. 1980, Sch. 7, para. 6(2).

dispute between a Minister whose consent is required (e.g. as highway authority for a trunk road) and a local authority as to whether the consent of that Minister is being unreasonably withheld is to be settled by arbitration.

Where a shelter is situated so as to obstruct access to telecommunication apparatus belonging to a telecommunications operator, or any sewer, pipe-subway, pipe, wire or other apparatus belonging to or maintained by a local authority or statutory undertaker, and the telecommunications operator or the authority or undertaker concerned gives notice requiring such access, the council shall temporarily remove the shelter or shall be liable to repay the extra expense incurred in obtaining access.[1] In view of this provision, and of statutory provisions imposing penalties for obstructing fire hydrants,[2] care should be taken in siting bus shelters to avoid obstructing access to any such apparatus.

Planning permission is not in general required for the erection of a bus shelter. (*See* "Planning Permission".)

A parish council may maintain shelters, or queue barriers or posts provided by them under Defence Regulations or without statutory powers, or accepted as a gift prior to the 14th July 1953.[3] The provisions with regard to consents and obstructions to access are applied to the maintenance of such shelters or barriers, subject to the modification that any necessary consent need not be obtained again if it was obtained when the shelter was first provided.

A parish council may borrow money for the provision of a

---

[1] L.G.(M.P.)A. 1953, s. 6, as amended by Telecommunications Act 1984, Sch. 4.
[2] Fire Services Act 1947, s. 14(5).
[3] L.G.(M.P.)A. 1953, s. 7.

bus shelter, subject to the usual consents. (*See* "Loans to Parish Councils".)

# BY-ELECTIONS

**(See Election and Appointment of Parish Councillors)**

# BY-LAWS

**(See *also* Baths and Wash-Houses—Mortuaries and Post-Mortem Rooms—Open Spaces—Recreation—Village Greens)**

A parish council may make by-laws for the following purposes:–

(i) the regulation of any pleasure ground or public walk, which is for the time being under its control, or to the expense of which it has contributed. The by-laws may provide for the removal from such ground, etc. of any person infringing any by-law, by any officer of the parish council or by a constable;[1]

(ii) the regulation of any open space or burial ground over which the parish council has acquired any interest or control by virtue of the Open Spaces Act 1906, including the days or times of admission thereto and the preservation of order and prevention of nuisances therein. The by-laws may provide for the removal of any person infringing any by-law by an officer of the parish council or by a constable;[2]

(iii)the regulation of any baths, swimming pools, bathing

---

[1] P.H.A. 1875, s. 164, and L.G.A. 1972, Sch. 14, para. 27.
[2] O.S.A. 1906, s. 15.

places or wash-houses provided by the parish council,[1] and swimming pools and bathing places not managed by the council and which are open to the public at a charge;[2] and the regulation of public bathing;[3]

(iv) the regulation of any mortuaries and post-mortem rooms provided by the parish council;[4]

(v) the regulation of the hiring of pleasure boats in a park or pleasure ground provided or managed by the council;[5]

(vi) to control dogs and dog fouling.[6]

Model by-laws for these purposes have been issued by central government. Inquiries should be made to Communities and Local Government, Byelaws Section, Eland House (3/J5), Bressenden Place, London SW1E 5DU.

The procedure for making by-laws is as follows.[7] By-laws are made under the hands and seals of two members of the parish council. They have no effect, however, until confirmed by the confirming authority, i.e. the Secretary of State. At least one month before application for confirmation, notice must be given of the intention to apply for confirmation, in one or more local newspapers. A copy of the by-laws must be deposited at the council offices, and be open to public inspection, without payment, for at least a month before application for confirmation.

---

[1] P.H.A. 1936, s. 223.

[2] P.H.A. 1936, s. 233.

[3] P.H.A. 1936, s. 231, as amended by L.G.(M.P.)A. 1976, s. 17, and L.G.A. 1972, Sch. 14, para. 18.

[4] P.H.A. 1936, s. 198.

[5] P.H.A.A.A. 1890, s. 44(2); P.H.A. 1961, s. 54.

[6] This power has been largely superseded by the C.N.A.E.A. 2005; see "Dog Control Orders".

[7] L.G.A. 1972, s. 236.

The council must on application furnish to any person a copy of the draft by-laws, or any part thereof, on payment of such sum, not exceeding 10p for every hundred words, as it may determine.

A copy of the confirmed by-laws must be printed and deposited at the council offices and open at all reasonable hours to public inspection without payment, and a copy must be furnished on application to any person, on payment of such sum not exceeding 20p for every copy as the council may determine.

By-laws may also be made on matters for which a local council has no direct authority, e.g. against cycling on footpaths,[1] by a district council or a unitary council. A parish council could ask that council to process such a by-law on its behalf or to delegate to the parish council the power to make it.[2]

Copies of any by-laws made by the above council must be transmitted to the clerk of the parish council of every local area to which such by-laws relate. In the case of a parish in England without a council, the copy must be sent to the chairman of the parish meeting. The copy of these by-laws must be deposited with the public documents of the local areas and must be open to public inspection, without payment, at all reasonable times.

## CAMPING AND CARAVANS

District councils and unitary councils in England and county and county borough councils in Wales have the

---

[1] L.G.A. 1972, s. 235.
[2] L.G.A. 1972, s. 101.

power to prohibit the parking of caravans on commons.[1] It is unlawful for caravans to be parked on a village green. (*See* "Village Greens".)

Visiting touring caravans may not, in general, be parked on private land without a licence from the above council, but a single van may be parked without a licence for not more than two nights. A licence is not necessary for the parking of a limited number of vans if the site is approved by a recognised organisation such as the Caravan Club.

## CAPITAL GAINS TAX

### (See Income Tax)

## CAR PARKS

### (See Parking Places)

## CASH

### (See Accounts)

## CASTING VOTE

### (See Chairman of Parish Council—Chairman of Parish Meeting)

## CASUAL VACANCY IN PARISH COUNCIL

### (See Election and Appointment of Parish Councillors)

---

[1] Caravan Sites and Control of Development Act 1960, s. 23, and L.G.A. 1972, Sch. 29, para. 14.

# CEMETERIES
### (See Burial and Cremation)

# CHAIRMAN OF PARISH COUNCIL
### (*See also* Chairman of Parish Meeting)

Each year the parish council at the commencement of its annual meeting is required to elect the chairman of the council.[1] If the council is a town council, he is entitled to the style of Town Mayor.[2] His election must be the first business transacted. The chairman must be elected from the members of the council. At the meeting at which the chairman is elected (or before or at a later meeting, if so permitted by the council) he must make in the presence of a member of the council, or the clerk of the council, and deliver to the council, a declaration of acceptance of office in the form prescribed which includes an undertaking to observe the council's code of conduct in the performance of his duties.[3] If he fails to do so, his office thereupon automatically becomes vacant. The chairman continues in office unless he resigns or becomes disqualified, until his successor becomes entitled to act as chairman. During his term of office the chairman continues to be a member of the council, notwithstanding that he may not have been re-elected as a councillor. If this happens, he only has a casting vote on the election of the new chairman.[4]

As to disqualifications for being chairman, *see* "Disqualifications for Office of Parish Councillor".

---

[1] L.G.A. 1972, ss. 15 and 34.
[2] L.G.A. 1972, s. 245.
[3] L.G.A. 1972, s. 83(4), as amended by L.G.H.A. 1989; L.G.A. 2000, s. 52(2). Form available from Shaw & Sons Ltd.
[4] L.G.A. 1972, s. 15(2).

A parish council may pay the chairman for the purpose of enabling him to meet the expenses of his office such allowance as the council thinks reasonable.[1] Provided the amount paid is a reasonable reimbursement for expenses actually incurred, the allowance is not taxable. The amount must not, however, include any element of remuneration for the chairman. In England, as an alternative, the chairman may be paid a parish basic allowance (*see* "Allowances to parish councillors").

The chairman may resign office by giving notice in writing to the council.[2] No acceptance by the council is necessary when the chairman sends in his resignation; the office becomes vacant on the receipt of notice of the resignation by the council.

The chairman of the parish council may convene a meeting of the council[3] or a parish meeting[4] at any time. He may also be required to heed a request for him to call a meeting by councillors (*see* "Meetings of Parish Council"). Public notice of any parish meeting and of any parish council meeting must be given, and in the latter case a summons, signed by the clerk, must also be sent to each councillor. Seven "clear days" means days exclusive of the day of notice and the day of the meeting. (*See* "Notices".)

Where the voting at a meeting of the parish council is equal, the chairman, or the person presiding in his place, has a second or casting vote.[5]

The minutes of a council meeting must be signed at the same or the next ensuing meeting by the presiding

---

[1]  L.G.A. 1972, ss. 15(5) and 34(5).

[2]  L.G.A. 1972, s. 84.

[3]  L.G.A. 1972, Sch. 12, para. 9(1) and 25(1).

[4]  *ibid.*, para. 15(1)(a) and 30(1)(a).

[5]  *ibid.*, para. 39(2).

chairman.[1] Any instrument to be executed by the council may be signed by the clerk on the council's behalf,[2] but if it is a document which requires a seal (e.g. a deed), it must be signed and sealed by two members of the council.[3]

Any notice required by law to be given to the chairman may be left at, or sent by post to, the offices of the council. (*See* "Notices".)

If the chairman of the parish council is present at any meeting, he must preside.[4]

The council may, if it thinks fit, appoint one of its number to be vice-chairman.[5] He holds office until immediately after the election of a chairman at the next annual meeting of the council, and during that time continues to be a member of the council for all purposes, notwithstanding that he may not have been re-elected as a councillor. The vice-chairman, in the absence or during the inability of the chairman to act, has all the powers and authority of the chairman; and, subject to any standing orders of the council, anything authorised to be done by, to, or before the chairman, may be done by, to, or before the vice-chairman.

## CHAIRMAN OF PARISH MEETING

If the chairman of the parish council is present at a parish meeting, he is the chairman of the meeting. If, in England, he is absent, the vice-chairman (if any) shall, if present, preside. If neither is present, the meeting may appoint a

---

[1]  L.G.A. 1972, Sch. 12, para. 41(1).
[2]  L.G.A. 1972, s. 234.
[3]  L.G.A. 1972, ss. 14(3) and 33(3).
[4]  L.G.A. 1972, Sch. 12, paras. 11(1) and 27(1).
[5]  L.G.A. 1972, ss. 15(6) and 34(6).

person to take the chair, and that person will then have the powers and authority of the chairman for the purpose of that meeting.[1]

In Wales, the office of vice-chairman of the community council does not entitle the person holding that office to be chairman of the community meeting if the chairman of the council is absent, although in practice he would no doubt take the chair unless the meeting decided otherwise.

In England, where a parish does not have a separate parish council, the parish meeting shall, subject to the provisions of a grouping order, at its annual assembly elect a chairman who will then, unless he resigns in writing, remain in office for the year.[2] The chairman continues in office until his successor is appointed. A casual vacancy in the office of chairman of the parish meeting is to be filled by the parish meeting.[3] In Wales, where a community does not have a separate community council, the meeting must appoint a chairman for the occasion only.[4]

Where the voting at a meeting is equal, the chairman has a second or casting vote.[5] A poll may be demanded before the conclusion of a meeting, on any question arising thereat. (*See* "Polls".)

Any notice required to be given to or served on a parish meeting may be given to or served on the chairman of the meeting.[6]

---

[1] L.G.A. 1972, Sch. 12, paras. 17 and 33.
[2] L.G.A. 1972, s. 15(10).
[3] L.G.A. 1972, s. 88(3).
[4] L.G.A. 1972, Sch. 12, para. 33.
[5] *ibid.*, paras. 18(3) and 34(3).
[6] L.G.A. 1972, s. 231(2).

## CHAPELS

### (See Burial and Cremation)

## CHARITIES

The law relating to charities is mainly to be found in the Charities Act 1993 and the Charities Act 2006. At the time of publication, not all of the 2006 Act was in force.

A parochial charity is one where the benefits (or a separate distribution of benefits) are confined to inhabitants of the parish which includes the area of the present civil parish (or part of it) or of an area consisting of the parish with not more than four neighbouring parishes.[1]

The parish council (or in some cases, in England only, the parish meeting) may by statute appoint trustees for certain parochial charities, in the circumstances listed below.[2] These powers are in addition to any powers of appointment conferred by a trust instrument. In no case do these include ecclesiastical charities. The circumstances are:–

(a) where before 1894 the inhabitants of the parish, the vestry or select vestry appointed trustees for (or beneficiaries of) a charity, the parish council shall appoint the trustees (or the persons who shall select the beneficiaries of the charity);

(b) where the churchwardens as such (before 1894) or the overseers as such (before 1927) were trustees, then the parish council shall appoint trustees to a not greater number than the former trustees;

(c) where the charity trustees of a charity not founded

[1] Ch.A. 1993, s. 96(1).
[2] Ch.A. 1993, s. 79(2) and (5).

within the preceding 40 years do not include persons elected by the electors, ratepayers or inhabitants or appointed by the parish council or parish meeting, the parish council or parish meeting may appoint such number of additional trustees as the Charity Commission may allow;

(d) where, in a case covered by (c) above, there is a sole charity trustee not so elected or appointed, the number of trustees may (with the approval of the Commission) be increased to three, one of the new trustees being appointed by the existing trustee and one by the parish council or parish meeting.

The term of office of first trustees appointed under these provisions is four years, except that where new appointments are made under (c) or (d) above and more than one trustee is appointed, half (as nearly as may be) must be for two years; and an appointment to fill a casual vacancy does not extend beyond the end of the term of the appointment it fills. Retiring trustees are eligible for re-appointment.[1]

Where trustees are appointed by the parish council, the council cannot itself administer the parochial charity. The trustees are an entirely different body from the parish council. Councillors may be appointed by the council as trustees, but if so they are acting as trustees, not as councillors.

The Act provides a valuable protection for a trustee in doubt as to how to execute his trust, in entitling him (on written application) to the advice of the Charity Commission.[2] The address of the Charity Commission is PO Box 1227, Liverpool L69 6UG. If he follows this he is

---

[1] Ch.A. 1993, s. 79(6).
[2] Ch.A. 1993, s. 29 (as substituted by Ch.A. 2006, s. 24).

protected against any action for breach of trust unless the matter had already been before the court or proceedings were pending, or he had reason to suspect that the advice was given in ignorance of material facts.

The Act also provides for co-operation between charities and the council.[1] Where the charity is established for a purpose similar or complementary to one of the council's services, the council may (if both parties wish) make arrangements with the charity for co-ordinating their work in the interest of the people served.

Trustees holding property for the purposes of a public recreation ground, or of allotments for the benefit of the inhabitants of the parish, or for any other charitable or public purposes connected with a parish – except for an ecclesiastical charity – may, with the approval of the Charity Commission, transfer the property to the parish council or to persons appointed by the council.[2] If the parish council accepts the transfer, the property will be held on the same trusts and subject to the same conditions as those under which the trustees held it.

The Act further provides for a change in the area to which a charity relates in certain cases where the original area is no longer appropriate.[3]

Where a charity is administered by a parish council, the accounts of the parochial charity are usually audited by the council's auditor. Where, however, the council only appoints trustees of the charity, but does not itself administer it, the accounts of the charity are distinct from those of the parish council, and will neither form part of its accounts nor be subject to audit by the auditor.

---

[1] Ch.A. 1993, s. 78.
[2] Ch.A. 1993, s. 79(1).
[3] Ch.A. 1993, s. 13(4).

The trustees of a charity are required to keep proper accounts and accounting records and must keep them for six years. The type of accounts to be kept are prescribed by regulations and depend upon the level of financial activity of the charity:–

1. For a non-company charity with a gross annual income not exceeding £250,000, accounts must be prepared, but may be on a receipts and payments basis, together with a statement of assets and liabilities.

2. For a non-company charity with a gross income exceeding £250,000 and all charitable companies, the accounts must be prepared on an accruals basis and must include a balance sheet, a statement of financial activities and explanatory notes.[1]

As a general rule, charities with a gross income between £25,000 and £500,000 are required to have their accounts examined by an independent examiner. Where a charity's gross income exceeds £500,000, a full audit is required. A full audit is also required where a charity's net liabilities exceed £3.6 million.

A trustee of a parochial charity, or his wife or children, cannot receive any benefit from the charity.

The draft of any scheme for the reform of an obsolete charity affecting the parish may be made by the Charity Commission and must be communicated to the parish council.[2] Charities may apply for a scheme to enable them to invest their funds jointly by setting up a common investment fund.[3]

---

[1] Ch.A. 1993, Part VI (as amended by Ch.A. 2006).
[2] Ch.A. 1993, s. 20 (as substituted by Ch.A. 2006, s. 22).
[3] Ch.A. 1993, s. 24.

All charities, apart from certain "exempt" charities and some "excepted" by regulation, *must* be registered by their trustees with the Charity Commission, unless, as a general rule, they have a gross annual income not exceeding £5,000. Charities with an income below this threshold may register voluntarily.[1] The effect of registration is to put beyond question the fact that the trust is charitable.

The Charities Act 1993 provides for the maintenance of local indexes of charities.[2] The indexes comprise extracts from the Central Register, maintained by the Charity Commissioners, covering charities which relate to the area of a local authority. The county council keeps an index and is entitled to free copies of any relevant entry in the Charity Commission's register. The county council has power to publish information contained in the index, and the index is open to public inspection. In county areas the index slips will be arranged according to the area in which the charity operates, so that where the area of benefit is made up of a number of parishes a separate slip will be found relating to each of the parishes.

The Act also provides for reviews of charities having the same or similar purposes to be made by county councils, but no charity can be reviewed without the consent of its trustees.[3]

For rating of charities, *see* "Rating and Valuation".

# CHEQUES

## (See Accounts)

---

[1] Ch.A. 1993, s. 3A (inserted by Ch.A 2006, s. 9).
[2] Ch.A. 1993, s. 76.
[3] Ch.A. 1993, s. 77.

## CHURCHYARDS

**(*See also* Closed Churchyards)**

Where a churchyard is open, a parish council may contribute towards its maintenance. (*See* "Burial and Cremation".)

## CITIZENS' ADVICE BUREAUX

A parish council may assist voluntary organisations to provide individuals with information about those individuals' rights and obligations. The council may also assist, by making or receiving communications or by providing representation before any person or body, in asserting those rights or fulfilling those obligations.[1]

In practice, this power is mostly used to provide financial assistance to Citizens' Advice Bureaux or similar organisations.

## CLERK OF PARISH COUNCIL

**(*See also* Agency—Deputy Officers—Employees— Gratuities to Officers—Legal Proceedings—Meetings of Parish Council—Parish Meeting—Superannuation of Paid Officers—Treasurer of Parish Council)**

A parish council must appoint such officers as it thinks necessary for the proper discharge of its functions.[2] In addition, a parish council must secure that one of its officers has responsibility for the administration of its financial affairs.[3] (*See* "Treasurer of Parish Council".) Thus a parish council may have an "executive and responsible

---

[1]  L.G.A. 1972, s. 142(2A).
[2]  L.G.A. 1972, s. 112.
[3]  L.G.A. 1972, s. 151, i.e. the responsible financial officer.

financial officer" but, in practice, all frequently falls upon the modest "clerk".

A member of the parish council may be appointed to be clerk of the council without remuneration,[1] but it is nowadays more usual for the council to appoint some other suitable person, not being a councillor, to the post and to pay him or her such reasonable remuneration as it may determine. A person who has been a parish councillor may not be appointed as clerk *with remuneration* until 12 months have elapsed since he ceased to be a councillor.[2] The appointment of a clerk or other parish council officer is made by resolution of the council.

Whilst few clerks are likely to take on the responsibilities purely for the money, a reasonable remuneration ought to be paid to every clerk. In recent years the status of clerks has considerably improved and all councils should be prepared to examine the payment made to their clerks in the light of the not inconsiderable work and responsibility which falls to them. Advice may be obtained from the Society of Local Council Clerks, 8 The Crescent, Taunton, Somerset TA1 4EA.

Certain functions of the council must be carried out by the proper officer of the council which means the officer specifically appointed for that purpose. For most matters this will be the clerk, but when a council has more than one officer, for example a separate treasurer, that officer may well be appointed the proper officer for certain statutory purposes.

As proper officer, the clerk will be required to sign the summonses to attend meetings[3] (*see* "Meetings of Parish

---

[1]  L.G.A. 1972, s. 112(5).
[2]  L.G.A. 1972, s. 116.
[3]  L.G.A. 1972, Sch. 12, para. 10(2)(b).

Council") but he has no power to fix the meetings of the council except in so far as he has the express or implied authority of the chairman to do so. The extent of his general authority over the council's affairs is governed by the wishes of the council.

The duties of the clerk will depend on the terms of his contract if he is an employee but will ordinarily include the duty of summoning and attending the meetings of the council; keeping the council minutes; taking charge of the council books and deeds and documents, and giving copies or extracts from the same to any person entitled, on payment of the prescribed or other reasonable charge for the same. If no separate treasurer is appointed he will also keep the accounts of the council and attend at the audit as may be required. As to whether it is part of his duty to take the minutes at parish meetings, *see* "Parish Meeting".

Service of any notice upon a parish council may be effected by service upon the office of the authority,[1] i.e. in practice, its clerk.

As to deposit of documents with the clerk, see "Books and Documents".

An officer must not, under colour of his office or employment, exact or accept any fee or reward whatsoever other than his proper remuneration,[2] although he is entitled to be reimbursed for all legitimate expenses.

If it comes to the knowledge of an officer that a contract in which he has any pecuniary interest, whether direct or indirect (not being a contract to which he is himself a party), has been, or is proposed to be, entered into by the

[1]  L.G.A. 1972, s. 231.
[2]  L.G.A. 1972, s. 117(2).

council or any committee of the council, he must as soon as practicable give notice in writing of his interest to the council.[1] An officer is treated as having an indirect interest if he would have been so treated had he been a member. On this, *see* "Interest in Contract or Other Matters".

An officer of the council has no personal liability in respect of anything done *in good faith* for the purpose of any of the council's statutory functions.[2]

As an employee of the council, the clerk is covered by the legislation (now very extensive) dealing with employment rights, discrimination in employment, unfair dismissal, redundancy and similar matters (*see* "Employees").

A national training strategy for clerks has been in existence since November 2001. Details can be obtained from the Society of Local Council Clerks (address above).

## CLOCKS

### (See Public Clocks)

## CLOSED CHURCHYARDS

### England

Any inhabitant of a parish, whatever his religion, is entitled to be buried in the churchyard.[3] Thus, if a churchyard ceases to be usable, the Secretary of State may make representations to the Privy Council for an Order in Council discontinuing burials in a churchyard where he is satisfied that such a step is necessary for the protection of

---

[1] L.G.A. 1972, s. 117(1).
[2] L.G.(M.P.)A. 1976, s. 39.
[3] *Hughes v. Lloyd* (1888) 22 Q.B.D. 157.

public health.[1] The parochial church council is responsible for the maintenance of the closed churchyard in decent order and for the necessary repairs to walls and fences.[2]

The parochial church council can at any time give three months' written notice to the parish council that it wishes the churchyard to be maintained at public expense.[3]

If the parish council prefers that the responsibility for maintenance should fall upon the district council rather than itself, it may within the three months so resolve and serve a further notice to this effect in writing upon the district council and the parochial church council. The district council is then obliged to take over the maintenance of the churchyard instead of the parish council at the end of the three months.[4]

If it does not serve the further notice, the parish council will become responsible for the maintenance of the churchyard at the end of the three months, and the parish council cannot thereafter transfer the responsibility to the district council.

As a consequence of the Care of Churches and Ecclesiastical Jurisdiction Measure 1991 (in force from 1st March 1993), the responsibility for maintaining trees in a closed churchyard now falls on the council.

A parish council cannot be required to maintain a churchyard which is disused but not closed.

### Wales

Before 1st April 1974, responsibility for the maintenance of

---

[1] Burial Act 1853, s. 1.
[2] L.G.A. 1972, s. 215(1).
[3] L.G.A. 1972, s. 215(2).
[4] L.G.A. 1972, s. 215(3).

closed churchyards could be transferred to the then parish councils and parish meetings. Any transfers which took place before that date remain effective. After that date, parishes were replaced by communities and the transfer procedure in section 215 of the Local Government Act 1972 does not apply in Wales. Community councils cannot therefore be required to take over maintenance of a closed churchyard. They may, however, contribute towards the cost incurred by any other person in so doing.[1]

The Care of Churches etc. Measure 1991 (*see above*) does not apply to the Church in Wales.

## CODE OF CONDUCT

Every parish council is required to adopt a code of conduct, which must contain the mandatory provisions of the model code of conduct prescribed by the Secretary of State.[2] (In fact, all the provisions of the model code are mandatory.) Every member and co-opted member of a parish council must comply with the council's code of conduct. The prescribed form of declaration of acceptance of office which every newly elected or co-opted councillor must sign contains an undertaking to observe the code. The model codes for English and Welsh councils are set out in Appendices 1 and 2.

Where a member has a prejudicial interest, he must withdraw from the room where the meeting is being held, unless he has been granted a dispensation by the standards committee of the "responsible authority" (i.e. the district

---

[1] L.G.A. 1972, s. 214(6).
[2] L.G.A 2000, s. 50; Local Authorities (Model Code of Conduct) Order 2007 (S.I. 1159); Local Authorities (Model Code of Conduct) (Wales) Order 2008 (S.I. 788).

or unitary county council in England and the county or county borough council in Wales). A dispensation will in general only be granted where the parish council would otherwise be unable to come to a decision (e.g. where so many councillors have prejudicial interests that the council is inquorate).

Every principal authority must establish a standards committee. The general functions of the standards committee are to promote and maintain high standards of conduct by members and to assist members to observe the council's code of conduct. The standards committee of the relevant principal authority (district or unitary council in England; county or county borough council in Wales) performs the foregoing general functions in relation to the parish councils in the authority's area. Every such standards committee must include at least one parish or community councillor and at least one such councillor must be present at a standards committee meeting when matters relating to the parish councils in the area are under consideration.

It is open to anyone to make a written allegation to the Standards Board (in England) (*see* "Standards Board") or the Public Services Ombudsman in Wales that a councillor has failed to observe the council's code of conduct.[1] An elaborate procedure is laid down for dealing with allegations of breaches of a council's code, the details of which are outside the scope of this book. If an allegation of breach of the code is proved, the councillor in question may be suspended or partially suspended (i.e. suspended only from performing particular functions or having particular responsibilities) for a period not exceeding one year or for the remainder of his term of office, if shorter. Alternatively, the councillor may be disqualified from office for up to five years.

---

[1] L.G.A. 2000, ss. 58 and 69.

# COMMISSION FOR LOCAL ADMINISTRATION

A parish council in England is not subject to inquiry by the Local Commissioner for Administration (the Local Government Ombudsman), nor can it instigate an inquiry into any other local authority. Any such complaint has to be made by an individual person, who may complain to the Local Commissioner or to an elected member of that authority. The address of the Commission is PO Box 4771, Coventry CV4 0EH (www.lgo.org.uk).

In Wales, a community council is subject to the jurisdiction of the Public Services Ombudsman for Wales. He can investigate complaints of maladministration and failures to provide a proper service in carrying out statutory functions. He also performs the functions which in England are performed by the Standards Board (*see* "Standards Board"). The address of the Public Services Ombudsman for Wales is 1 Fford yr Hen Gae, Pencoed CF35 5LJ (www.ombudsman-wales.org.uk).

# COMMITTEES

## (See *also* Joint Committees—Parish Meeting—Standards Committee)

A parish council may arrange to discharge any of its functions through a committee, or a sub-committee, of the council.[1] In the view of the author, there is no reason why such a committee should not include all the members of the council, if that is the wish of the council, but an executive committee of one is illegal.[2] Unless the council

---

[1] L.G.A. 1972, s. 101.

[2] *R. v. Secretary of State for the Environment ex parte Hillingdon London Borough Council* [1986] 2 All E.R. 273. It follows that the chairman can exercise no executive action on behalf of the council.

otherwise directs, any committee appointed by the council may itself arrange for the discharge of any of its functions by a sub-committee. It is not necessary for the full council to ratify committee decisions. The only powers which cannot be transferred to a committee are those of issuing a precept for a rate and of borrowing money. A committee (other than a finance committee) may include persons who are not members of the parish council.[1]

Special rules for committees of local councils are to be found in the Parish and Community Councils (Committees) Regulations 1990 (S.I. 2476). These provide that non-councillor members of a committee have a vote in the following cases: (a) where the committee manages, within a budget set by the council, land or buildings occupied by the council (e.g. a village hall); (b) where the committee is a harbour authority; (c) where the committee performs functions relating to tourism; and (d) where the committee, within a budget set by the council, performs functions relating to the management of a festival. Every member of a committee who at the time of his appointment was a member of the parish council, upon ceasing to be a councillor, ceases also to be a member of the committee or sub-committee.[2]

If the parish council has any functions which are to be discharged in a part only of the parish, or in relation to a recreation ground, building, or property held for the benefit of a part only of the parish, the council may appoint a committee for that function.

Any arrangement made by a parish council for the discharge of any of its functions by a committee or sub-committee does not prevent the council or committee which made the arrangements from exercising these functions.

---

[1] L.G.A. 1972, s. 102(3), as amended by L.G.H.A. 1989, s. 13(8).
[2] L.G.A. 1972, s. 102(5).

A parish council may also appoint an advisory committee in respect of any matter relating to the discharge of any of its functions and there are no restrictions on membership of such committees. In fact it may consist entirely of non-members.[1] (*See* "Standing Orders".)

The parish council may make, vary and revoke standing orders respecting the quorum, proceedings and place of meeting of a committee or (with the other authorities concerned) a joint committee but, subject to any such standing orders, the quorum, proceedings and place of meeting shall be such as the committee or joint committee determine.[2] (*See* "Standing Orders".)

The public (which includes members of the Press) must be admitted to all committees of the parish council. In the case of sub-committees, there is no obligation to admit the public, but it is advisable to do so since the public and the Press have a legitimate interest in the deliberations and decisions of all local authorities. (For exclusion of the public, see "Meetings of Parish Council".)

The chairman at any meeting of a committee or a joint committee has a second or casting vote.

Minutes of the proceedings of every committee must be kept. They should be submitted to the parish council, but only require the council's approval in so far as they relate to the exercise of powers or functions of the council which have not been transferred to the committee. (*See* "Inspection of Documents".)

The accounts of a committee form part of the accounts of the parish council and are to be audited as part of

---

[1] L.G.A. 1972, s. 102(4).
[2] L.G.A. 1972, s. 106.

those accounts. For audit of joint committees, *see* "Joint Committees".

## COMMON PASTURE

Where it appears desirable to acquire land for affording common pasture, a parish council may prepare and carry into effect a scheme for acquiring such land, provided that the land can be acquired at such price or rent that all expenses incurred may reasonably be expected to be recouped out of the charges paid in respect thereof.[1] Upon such a scheme being carried into effect, the statutory provisions relating to allotments (e.g. the making of rules) will apply in like manner as if "allotments" in those provisions included common pasture, and "rent" included a charge for turning out an animal on the pasture. (*See* "Allotments".) Rules made by the parish council in respect of common pasture may extend to regulating the turning out of animals on the common pasture, defining the persons entitled to turn them out, the number to be turned out, and the conditions under which animals may be turned out, and fixing the charges to be made for each animal, and otherwise for regulating the management of the common pasture.

## COMMONS

### (*See also* Roadside Wastes—Village Greens)

Common land is land subject to rights of common, or manorial waste, registered as common land under the Commons Registration Act 1965 or the Commons Act 2006. For the purposes of the 1965 and 2006 Acts, the term common land excludes village greens (although the

---

[1] S.H.A.A. 1908, s. 34, as amended by L.G.A. 1972, Sch. 29, para. 9.

latter were, and are, also registrable under the Acts as a separate category). In earlier statutes, however, references to common land may be taken as including village greens. Registration under the 1965 Act has been completed. The 2006 Act will, when fully in force, introduce an updated system of registration to ensure that the registers are kept up to date, as well as making provision for new registrations. The registration provisions of the 2006 Act will be brought into force on a regional basis, following the successful completion of pilot projects in selected areas. Pilot projects are taking place in Devon, Kent (except unitary council areas in these counties), Cornwall, Hertfordshire, Herefordshire, Lancashire (except Blackpool), and Blackburn and Darwen. The whole of England is likely to be covered by 2013. The timetable for Wales is not yet known.

There are powers to prevent the unlawful inclosure of commons. These can be exercised in England by anyone, including a parish council. In Wales, those powers are effectively restricted to county and county borough councils.[1]

A parish council which owns common land should be cautious in purporting to allow any person or body to do anything which may be unlawful. For example, a building or fencing of any kind on land subject to rights of common is unlawful without the consent of the Secretary of State.[2] Any person who camps or lights a fire on common land, or who drives a vehicle on to it, commits an offence if the common land is subject to section 193 of the Law of Property Act 1925. In addition it is, in any event, an

---

[1] C.A. 2006, Part 3 (England); L.P.A. 1925, s. 194 (Wales). At the date of publication, Part 3 of the C.A. 2006 had not been brought into force in Wales.

[2] C.A. 2006, Part 3 (England); L.P.A. 1925, s. 194 (Wales).

offence to drive a car on to a common more than 15 yards from the road,[1] although if the parish council owns the common, or can obtain the permission of the owner, a simpler expedient against unwanted parking is to dig a ditch or place large white stones on the boundary.

Under section 61 of the Criminal Justice and Public Order Act 1994, powers are given to the police to remove trespassers from land, if the trespassers are there for the purpose of residence (e.g. "travellers"). The power is exercisable if the trespassers have caused damage, or have used threatening, abusive or insulting words to the occupier, or if they have six or more vehicles with them on the land. The section applies specifically to common land. Where the public has access to such land, the local authority is treated as an occupier and may therefore ask the police to remove the trespassers. The local authority is the parish council, the district council, the county council or the unitary council; they have concurrent powers in this respect.[2]

A parish council may agree to contribute the whole or any portion of the expense of a scheme prepared by the district or unitary council for the regulation and management of any common within a parish or community under the Commons Act 1899.[3] Powers to make a scheme or to confer powers of management under such a scheme may be transferred to the parish council by the district council.[4]

Where common land is registered but has no registered owner, a parish council (and any other local authority

---

[1] R.T.A. 1988, s. 34.

[2] C.J.P.O.A. 1994, ss. 61, 62.

[3] Commons Act 1899, s. 5 but note the possibility of the powers of the district council being taken over by the county council if there is no longer a district council.

[4] L.G.A. 1972, s. 101.

in the area of which the common is situated) has power to protect the common from unlawful interference (e.g. trespass or encroachment) and may take legal proceedings for this purpose.[1]

A right of public access on foot extends to all registered common land under Part 1 of the Countryside and Rights of Way Act 2000.

## COMMUNITY

### Wales

In Wales, all rural parishes in existence immediately before 1st April 1974 ceased to exist as local areas, but were reborn on that date under the name of communities. This name was also given in Wales to all former boroughs and urban districts in existence immediately before 1st April 1974, with a few adjustments involving some grouping of divided parts of former urban districts.[2]

Thus every part of Wales lies within a local area known as a community, in contrast to England where the effect of the change was that only the former rural parishes and certain free-standing urban areas constitute the comparable local area known as a parish (*see* "Parish").

There is a right to convene a community meeting for any community in Wales (*see* "Parish Meeting"). A community meeting is not a corporate body and in most cases where there is no council, property is held on its behalf by the county or county borough council. (To compare the position in this respect in England, *see* "Parish Trustees".) Unless it is specifically stated to the contrary or the

---

[1]   C.A. 2006, s. 45.
[2]   L.G.A. 1972, s. 20.

context indicates otherwise, any reference in this book to a "parish" should be taken as including a "community", and any reference to a "parish meeting" should be taken as including a "community meeting". It is hoped that Welsh readers will in no way take this amiss. It is done simply for ease and economy of expression.

**England**

In England, a parish may style itself a "community", "neighbourhood" or "village". (*See* "Name and Style of Parish".)

## COMMUNITY CENTRES

### (*See* Village Halls)

## COMMUNITY COUNCIL

### (*See* Parish Council)

## COMMUNITY GOVERNANCE REVIEWS

### (*See* Alteration of Areas)

## COMMUNITY MEETING

### (*See* Community—Parish Meeting)

## COMPULSORY PURCHASE OF LAND

### (*See also* Property of Parish Council)

In some cases, there are specific powers enabling parish councils to compulsorily purchase land for certain functions, e.g. allotments,[1] but generally if a parish council is unable to acquire by agreement and on reasonable terms suitable land for *any* purpose for which it is authorised to acquire land it may represent the case to the district or unitary council, and if that council is satisfied that suitable land cannot be purchased on reasonable terms by agreement, and that the circumstances are such as to justify it in proceeding with a view to compulsory purchase, it must hold a local inquiry into the representation of the parish council.[2] The district or unitary council is required to publish in the parish, in the manner prescribed[3] by the Secretary of State, notice of the inquiry and also to serve notice in the prescribed form on the owners, lessees and occupiers of the land proposed to be taken. After the inquiry has been completed and all objections by persons interested have been considered, the district or unitary council may make a compulsory purchase order, which cannot become effective until it is confirmed by the Secretary of State. The confirmed order is carried out by the district or unitary council, but the land itself is conveyed to the parish council.

If the district or unitary council refuses to make an order for the purchase of the land otherwise than by agreement, the parish council may petition the Secretary of State, who may, after holding a local inquiry, make a compulsory purchase order.

This power of a parish council to acquire compulsorily any land which is necessary for any of its functions is quite general. It is not limited by the fact that particular statutes confer powers of compulsory acquisition on local authorities except parish councils.

---

[1] S.H.A.A. 1908, ss. 25, 39.

[2] L.G.A. 1972, s. 125, as substituted by H.P.A. 1986, s. 43.

[3] Compulsory Purchase of Land (Prescribed Forms) (Ministers) Regulations 2004, S.I. 2595.

The word "land" in relation to any purpose for which the parish council is authorised to acquire land includes any interest in land, and any easement or right in, to, or over land.

The procedure on compulsory acquisition is governed by the provisions of the Acquisition of Land Act 1981.

Under the provisions of the Land Compensation Act 1961, as amended by the Planning and Compensation Act 1991, the price payable to the owner on compulsory acquisition is broadly speaking the market value of the land, estimated by the district valuer and determined in the event of dispute by the Lands Tribunal, but advice should be taken on the latest legal position in this respect.

The district or unitary council may make an order for the compulsory purchase of land for the purpose of letting it to a parish council for allotments. Such an order is subject to confirmation by the Secretary of State. (*See* "Allotments".)

## CONCURRENT POWERS

All the powers of a parish council, with the exception of allotments in England, are concurrent with those of the district or unitary council.

## CONFERENCES

### England

There is no longer any specific provision for parish councils to pay expenses and allowances for attending conferences or meetings. If attendance at a conference or meeting is an "approved duty", expenses may be paid (*see* "Allowances to Parish Councillors – England").

## Wales

A community council may pay any councillor allowances for attendance at conferences or meetings. These allowances are attendance allowance or financial loss allowance and travelling and subsistence allowance (*see* "Allowances to Parish Councillors – Wales"). This applies to any conference or meeting which the council itself considers relates to the interests of its area or its inhabitants. The only exclusions are conferences which are convened in the course of trade or business or the objects of which are wholly or partly political. The council itself decides how many councillors may attend. There are no restrictions on the number of conferences which may be attended.[1]

Thus, any number of councillors may be authorised to attend meetings of County Associations and conferences of the National Association of Local Councils.

## CONSENT OF PARISH COUNCIL

Although there are now several cases where notice must be given to a council (*see* "Notices by or to Parish Council"), in the following case, the parish council is actually able to prevent another authority from carrying out a statutory function.

If a highway authority applies to a magistrates' court for authority to stop up or divert an unclassified road, including a footpath or bridleway, the highway authority must be able to satisfy the court that the relevant parish council has been advised and for a period of two months has not refused its consent. (*See* "Highways".)

It may also be noted here that no parish in England may be

---

[1]  L.G.A. 1972, s. 175.

grouped without the consent of the parish meeting of each of the parishes. (*See* "Grouping of Parishes".)

## CONSENTS, ETC. UNDER THE PARISH COUNCILS ACT 1957

### (*See also* Lighting—Parking Places—Public Clocks— Roadside Seats and Shelters)

The powers to provide roadside seats and shelters, public clocks and public lighting under the Parish Councils Act 1957 are subject to the provisions of that Act as to consents and access to telegraphic lines, etc.[1]

None of these things, nor any material or apparatus, is to be provided on any land or premises not forming part of a road or in a position obstructing or interfering with any existing access to any such land or premises, except with the consent of the owner and the occupier; or in any road which is not a highway or in any public path except with the consent of the owner and the occupier of land over which the road or path runs.

For the definition of "road", *see* "Roads".

Similarly, such provision in, or on land abutting on, any road which is a highway requires the consent of the highway authority (or the Secretary of State in the case of a trunk road or other road maintained by him). The consent of the undertakers concerned is also required where the provision is to be made in a road which is a highway belonging to and repairable by any railway, dock, harbour, canal, inland navigation or passenger road transport undertakers and forming the approach to any station, dock, wharf or depot

---

[1] P.C.A. 1957, s. 5.

of those undertakers; or on the approaches to any bridge carrying a highway over any railway, dock, harbour, canal or inland navigation, or under any bridge carrying a railway, canal or inland navigation over a highway.

Any of these consents is not to be unreasonably withheld but may be given subject to reasonable conditions, which may include a condition that the council shall subsequently remove the thing provided if reasonably required to do so. Any disputes are to be settled by the Secretary of State (who may hold a local inquiry for the purpose) or, where he is one of the parties, by arbitration.

The provisions of section 6 of the Local Government (Miscellaneous Provisions) Act 1953, relating to access to telecommunication apparatus, sewers, etc. in the case of bus shelters, are applied also by section 5 of the Act of 1957, to the exercise of these powers (*see* "Bus Shelters").

## CONSTABLES, PARISH

The office of parish constable was abolished by the Police Act 1964.

## CONSULTATION

### England

There is no specific requirement for principal authorities to consult parish councils on matters of common concern. The power of the Secretary of State to designate such matters, contained in the Local Government and Rating Act 1997 (a power which was never used), was abolished by the Local Government and Public Involvement in Health Act 2007. However, a considerable number of principal authorities have drawn up formal consultation agreements with the parishes in their areas; these are sometimes called "charters" (*see also* "Quality Parish Councils"). These agreements do not affect any statutory rights of consultation which parish councils may have (*see* "Planning"). The National Association of Local Councils has issued a good practice guide on charters.

**Wales**

The Local Government Act 1972[1] provides that the Secretary of State may designate matters on which principal councils must consult community councils in their area before a decision is made. No designations have yet been made. Instead, guidance is given in the joint publication of the Welsh Local Government Association, One Voice Wales and the Welsh Assembly Government entitled *Relationship Building and Charters for Unitary Authorities and Community and Town Councils*.

## CONTRACTS OF PARISH COUNCIL

**(See *also* Best Value—Interest in Contract or Other Matters—Officers of Parish Council—Standing Orders)**

A parish council may enter into any contracts which are relevant to the discharge of any of its functions.[2] Apart from contracts for the sale or other disposition of land, which must be made in writing,[3] contracts may legally be made in any form.

A parish council may also make standing orders with respect to the making of contracts by the council. However, it *must*

---

[1] L.G.A. 1972, s. 33A, inserted by L.G.W.A. 1994, s. 14.
[2] L.G.A. 1972, s. 111.
[3] L.P.(M.P.)A. 1989, s. 2.

make such orders with respect to contracts for the supply of goods or materials to the council, or for the carrying out of any works, which orders must include a provision for regulating the manner in which tenders are invited, but may exempt from any such provision contracts below a certain fixed price or generally where the council is satisfied that exemption is justified by special circumstances.[1]

Model standing orders are available from the National Association of Local Councils. (*See* "Standing Orders".)

## CONTRACT WITH THE COUNCIL, INTEREST IN

### (*See* Interest in Contracts or Other Matters)

## CONVENING OF MEETINGS

### (*See* Meetings of Parish Council—Parish Meeting)

## CO-OPTION

### (*See* Election and Appointment of Parish Councillors)

## CORPORATION TAX

A parish council is not liable to corporation tax.

## COUNCILLOR

### (*See* Parish Councillor)

---

[1]  L.G.A. 1972, s. 135.

## COUNCIL TAX

Council tax is the local tax payable in respect of the occupation of residential property. Parish councils, and parish meetings in England without a council, obtain most of their income by precepting on the billing authority (district or unitary council), which raises the money from the council tax payers in the parish area. Council tax bills show the amount raised in this way. (*See* "Precepts" and "Expenses and Expenditure".)

## COUNTY ASSOCIATION OF PARISH OR LOCAL COUNCILS

**(*See* National Association of Local Councils)**

## COUNTY COUNCIL, CONSENT OF

Many former restrictions on parish council powers in the nature of the need to obtain the consent of the county council have disappeared in recent years. Of the remaining ones, the most important relate to lighting powers (*see* "Lighting"), grass verges and traffic signs (*see* "Highways"), car parks (*see* "Parking Places") and public conveniences (*see* "Public Conveniences").

## CREMATION

**(*See* Burial and Cremation)**

## CRIME PREVENTION

A parish council may, for the detection or prevention of crime, (a) install and maintain any equipment (e.g. closed-circuit television cameras), (b) establish and maintain any scheme (e.g. neighbourhood watch) and (c) assist others in undertaking the foregoing. The council may also make grants to the police authority for police purposes.[1]

The responsible authorities for each local government area (primarily county councils and unitary authorities) and the police must formulate a strategy for the reduction of crime and disorder in their area. They must co-operate and share prescribed information with other bodies, including parish councils, in producing and implementing the strategy.[2] Parish councils must exercise their functions with due regard to the likely effect of such exercise on crime and disorder in their area and the need to prevent them.[3]

## CUSTODY OF BOOKS

**(See Books and Documents)**

## CYCLE PARKS

**(See Parking Places)**

## DAMAGE

Damages recoverable by the parish council or parish meeting for damage caused by negligence to any lamp, lamp-post, notice board, fence, rail, post, shelter or other

---

[1] L.G.R.A. 1997, s. 31.

[2] Crime and Disorder Act 1998, s. 5; Crime and Disorder Strategies (Prescribed Descriptions) (England) Order 2004 (S.I. 118); Crime and Disorder Strategies (Prescribed Descriptions) Order 1998 (S.I. 2452) (Wales); Crime and Disorder (Prescribed Information) Regulations 2007 (S.I. 1831).

[3] Crime and Disorder Act 1998, s. 17.

"apparatus or equipment provided by them in a street or public place" are recoverable in a magistrates' court as a civil debt if the amount does not exceed £20.[1] Above that figure proceedings should be taken in the county court.

On a prosecution for criminal damage, a magistrates' court can, on conviction, order the offender to pay up to £5,000 compensation in addition to any punishment inflicted.[2]

# DECLARATION OF ACCEPTANCE OF OFFICE

**(See Parish Councillor)**

# DECLARATION OF INTEREST

**(See Code of Conduct)**

# DECLARATION THAT HIGHWAY IS UNNECESSARY

**(See Highways)**

# DEDICATION OF HIGHWAY

**(See Highways)**

# DELEGATION

**(See Agency—Committees)**

---

[1] P.H.A. 1961, s. 81 and Powers of Criminal Courts (Sentencing) Act 2000, s. 131.
[2] Powers of Criminal Courts (Sentencing) Act 2000.

# DEPOSITORY FOR BOOKS

## (See Books and Documents)

# DEPUTY OFFICERS

As a consequence of its general power to appoint such officers as it thinks necessary,[1] a parish council which has appointed a clerk or treasurer may appoint a standing deputy of that officer, for the purpose of acting in his place whenever the office is vacant or the holder is unable to act. A deputy thus appointed will have, subject to the terms of his appointment, all the functions of the holder of the office. The parish council may pay a deputy officer, not being a member of the council, such reasonable sum as it may determine.

Similarly, if the office of clerk or treasurer is vacant, or the holder is unable to act, and no standing deputy has been appointed or, if appointed, is unable to act, the parish council may in such case appoint a temporary deputy to act in the vacant office; and, subject to the terms of his appointment, the person so appointed will have all the functions of the holder of the office. As in the case of a standing deputy, the council may pay a person appointed as temporary deputy officer, not being a member of the council, such reasonable remuneration as it may determine.

As to disclosure by an officer of his interest in any contract, *see* "Clerk of the Parish Council".

# DESTRUCTION OF BOOKS, ETC.

## (See Books and Documents)

---

[1] L.G.A. 1972, s. 112.

## DISCLOSURE OF INTEREST

### (See Code of Conduct)

## DISQUALIFICATIONS FOR OFFICE OF PARISH COUNCILLOR

### (See *also* Interest in Contract or Other Matters—Parish Councillor)

A person is disqualified for being elected or being a member of a parish council if he has, within five years before his election or since his election, been convicted of crime, and has had passed upon him a sentence of imprisonment (whether suspended or not) for a period of not less than three months without the option of a fine, or is subject to a bankruptcy restrictions order or an interim order or has made a composition or arrangement with his creditors; or holds any paid office or employment (other than the office of chairman or vice-chairman), the appointment to which is made or confirmed by the parish council, or by any committee of the council (including a joint committee), or by any employee of the council, or is disqualified under the provisions relating to corrupt or illegal practices.[1]

In addition, an adjudication panel or a case tribunal established under Part III, Chapter IV of the Local Government Act 2000 may disqualify a councillor for up to five years for failure to comply with the council's code of conduct[2] (*see* "Code of Conduct").

The disqualification by reason of bankruptcy dates from the judgment or execution and generally lasts for one year after the order is made.[3]

---

[1]   L.G.A. 1972, s. 80(1), as amended by L.G.F.A. 1982.
[2]   L.G.A. 2000, s. 79.
[3]   L.G.A. 1972, s. 81(1)(b), as substituted by the Enterprise Act 2002, s. 267(1).

A paid officer of a local authority who is employed under the direction of a committee or sub-committee, any member of which is appointed on the nomination of the parish council, is disqualified from being elected or being a member of the parish council.[1]

A person who is disqualified from being elected or being a member of the parish council is disqualified for being a member of a committee or sub-committee of the council, or for being a representative of the council on a joint committee appointed by agreement between the council and other local authorities.[2]

If a member fails throughout a period of six consecutive months from the date of his last attendance to attend any meeting of the council, he ceases to be a member of the council, unless the failure was due to some reason approved by the council *before* the expiry of that period. Approval cannot be given after the six-month period has expired. Absence due to service with the Armed Forces during war or any emergency does not in any event vacate the office. Attendance at a meeting of a committee or sub-committee of the council, or at a joint committee of the council and another local authority, is deemed to be attendance at a meeting of the council.[3]

When a member ceases to be qualified, or becomes disqualified for any reason other than by reason of a decision by a case tribunal under section 79 of the Local Government Act 2000, a conviction, or a breach of election laws, or ceases to be a member of the council by reason of failure to attend meetings, the council must forthwith

[1] L.G.A. 1972, s. 80(2).
[2] L.G.A. 1972, s. 104.
[3] L.G.A. 1972, s. 85.

declare the office vacant[1] and signify the vacancy by public notice. (*See* "Notices".)

Proceedings may be instituted, either in the High Court or in a magistrates' court, against any person acting as a member of a parish council who is disqualified from so acting.[2] Proceedings must be instituted before the expiration of six months from the date on which the person so acted. A magistrates' court can impose on the defendant to such proceedings a fine up to level 3 on the standard scale for summary offences (currently £1,000) for each occasion on which he has acted as a member of the council when disqualified. If, however, the court is satisfied that the matter would be more properly dealt with in the High Court, it must order a discontinuance of proceedings in the magistrates' court. The High Court's powers include the making of a declaration that the defendant is disqualified and that the office is vacant. An injunction may also be obtained restraining the defendant from continuing to act as if he were a member. Proceedings may not be instituted by any person other than a local government elector for the parish.

For the purposes of legal proceedings, a person is deemed to be disqualified for acting as a member of the parish council in the following cases:–

(a) if he is not qualified to be or is disqualified from being, a member of the council; or

(b) if, by reason of failure to make and deliver the declaration of acceptance of office within the period required, or by reason of resignation, or of failure to attend meetings of the council, he has ceased to be a member of the council.

---

[1]  L.G.A. 1972, s. 86.
[2]  L.G.A. 1972, s. 92.

The above provisions apply with the necessary modifications to the case of a disqualified person acting as a member of a committee or sub-committee of the parish council, or of a joint committee of which the parish council is one of the appointing authorities.

## DISSOLUTION OF PARISH OR COMMUNITY COUNCIL

### (See Parish Council)

## DISTURBANCES AT MEETINGS

### (See Meetings of Parish Council)

## DITCHES AND DRAINS

### (See *also* Nuisances—Sewerage)

A parish council may deal with any pond, pool, ditch, gutter or place containing, or used for the collection of, any drainage, filth, stagnant water, or matter likely to be prejudicial to health, by draining, cleansing or covering it, or otherwise preventing it from being prejudicial to health, but so as not to interfere with any private right, or with any public drainage, sewerage or sewage disposal works. Thus, for example, a parish council may clean out a village beck.

The parish council may execute any works, including works of maintenance, incidental to or consequential on any exercise of this power; and it may contribute towards the expenses incurred by any other person in doing any of the things mentioned above.[1] The council is not, however,

---

[1] P.H.A. 1936, s. 260.

directly empowered to take legal proceedings to enforce the abatement of any such nuisance. Where such a nuisance exists, the course to adopt is to bring the matter to the notice of the district or unitary council. If, however, the district council fails to act, the parish council has certain reserve powers (*see* "Nuisances").

At common law, there is a presumption that a roadside ditch belongs to the adjoining owner,[1] but it is a question of fact in each case. Highway authorities have the power but not a duty to clean such ditches.[2] However, the duty of highway authorities to repair and maintain highways extends to the provision of an adequate system of drainage.[3] Failure to provide this could result in an accident for which the highway authority would be liable.

## DIVERSION OF A HIGHWAY

### (See Highways)

## DOCUMENTS

### (See Books and Documents)

## DOG CONTROL ORDERS

Under the Clean Neighbourhoods and Environment Act 2005, Part 6, a parish council (called in the Act a "secondary authority") has power to make orders to control dogs.

A dog control order may relate to one or more of the following:

---

[1] *Hanscombe v. Bedfordshire County Council* [1938] 3 All E.R. 647.
[2] H.A. 1980, s. 100.
[3] *Burnside v. Emerson* [1968] 1 W.L.R. 1490.

(a) fouling of land by dogs and the removal of dog faeces;

(b) keeping of dogs on leads;

(c) exclusion of dogs from land;

(d) the number of dogs which a person may take on to any land.

Dog control orders may only apply to land in the open air to which the public are entitled or permitted to have access, with or without payment. Covered land is in the open air if it is open to the air on at least one side. The Secretary of State may designate land which is not to be subject to dog control orders. Forestry Commission land and land over which a road passes have been designated (these are covered by separate legislation).[1]

An authorised officer of a secondary authority may issue a fixed penalty notice where he has reason to believe an offence has been committed under a dog control order made by the authority. The officer may also issue a fixed penalty notice where he has reason to believe an offence has been committed under a dog control order made by a primary authority (district council, unitary council, Welsh county or county borough council). The amount of the fixed penalty is the amount specified by the authority (which may differ for different offences) or, if none, £75. The Secretary of State has power to prescribe maximum and minimum penalty amounts. In England, the Environmental Offences (Fixed Penalties) (Miscellaneous Provisions) Regulations 2007[2] prescribe £80 and £50 as the maximum and minimum amounts. In Wales, the Environmental Offences (Fixed

---

[1] Control on Dogs (Non-application to Designated Land) Order 2006 (S.I. 779); Control on Dogs (Non-application to Designated Land) (Wales) Order 2007 (S.I. 701).

[2] S.I. 175.

Penalties) (Miscellaneous Provisions) (Wales) Regulations 2007[1] prescribe £75 and £150 as those amounts.

Defra has issued guidance on dog control in its publication *Dog Control Orders*. It has also issued particular guidance to parish councils in its publication *Getting to grips with the Clean Neighbourhoods and Environment Act 2005 – a parish council guide to environmental enforcement.*

## DRAINAGE

### (See Ditches and Drains)

## EDUCATION

### England

A parish council in England no longer has a specific right to appoint a governor to a primary school. The right of parish councils in England to appoint a governor in certain cases was abolished by the Education Act 2002, although existing governors continued to hold office until, at the latest, 31st August 2006.

Under the Education Act 2002, the governing body of a maintained school consists of a number of different categories of governor, one of which is "community governor". Such a governor is defined as "(a) a person who lives or works in the community served by the school, or (b) a person who, in the opinion of the governing body, is committed to the good government and the success of the school".[2] Such persons could be parish councillors.

---

[1] S.I. 739.

[2] School Governance (Constitution) (England) Regulations 2007 (S.I. 957), Reg. 7.

## Wales

The Education Act 2002 applies in Wales and the general provisions relating to the appointment of governors are the same as for England. However, the instrument of government of a community, voluntary or foundation school which is a primary school and a maintained nursery school which serves the area of one or more community councils must provide for one community governor to be nominated by the community council. If the school serves the area of one of more community councils, the governors may seek nominations from one or more of those councils.[1]

For secondary schools, parish councils and parish meetings have no statutory right of appointment, but the local education authority may be persuaded to provide for the parish council or meeting to nominate a governor.

# ELECTION AND APPOINTMENT OF PARISH COUNCILLORS

**(See *also* Disqualifications for Office of Parish Councillor—Local Government Electors—Parish Councillor—Parish Meeting)**

## Election

Parish councillors are elected for a term of four years. They retire together on the fourth day after the date of the elections every four years. Their places are then filled by newly-elected councillors who come into office the same day.[2] A retiring councillor is eligible for re-election.

The term of office for a parish councillor is the same as

---

[1] Government of Maintained Schools (Wales) Regulations 2005 (S.I. 2914), Reg. 20.

[2] L.G.A. 1972, ss. 16(3) and 35(2).

that of the district or unitary councillor representing the same area. Consequently, in special cases where a district council changes from annual to triennial elections, or *vice versa*, the term of office of a parish councillor could, as a result, vary from the usual period.

Apart from what is stated in the Local Government Act 1972, the law relating to local council elections is now contained in the Representation of the People Acts 1983 and 1985, and local election rules made by the Secretary of State, i.e. the Local Elections (Parishes and Communities) (England and Wales) Rules 2006.[1]

The right to vote in local government elections depends upon the person's name having been entered in the current register of local government electors. The register is published annually not later than 1st December, following a canvas of persons in residence on 15th October. However, names may be added to or deleted from the register at any time during the year, thus creating a "rolling" register. This is intended to allow changes to be made at once, rather than on an annual basis as used to be the case. Those entitled to be registered as electors are those who are resident in the area and are British subjects,[2] citizens of the Republic of Ireland or citizens of a member state of the European Union of full age (18), or who will attain full age before the end of 12 months beginning with 1st December next, and are not subject to any legal incapacity to vote. (*See* "Local Government Electors".)

If the parish is divided into wards, there will be an election of parish councillors for each ward. (*See* "Wards".) A ward must lie wholly within the area of a district or unitary council ward.

---

[1] S.I. 3305.
[2] Which includes Commonwealth citizens.

The elections are held on the first Thursday in May, unless the Secretary of State, by order made not later than 1st February in the *preceding* year, fixes a different date.[1]

In all cases, the ordinary election of parish councillors is to be conducted by means of nomination of candidates by two electors and, if necessary, a poll.

Every district or unitary council must appoint an officer of the council to be the returning officer for the election of parish councillors within the district.[2] This may be a different officer from that appointed to be the returning officer for the election of district councillors. The returning officer may delegate all or any of his functions to any person, not necessarily being an officer of the district or unitary council.[3]

The poll is to begin at seven o'clock in the morning and is to be kept open until ten o'clock in the evening.

The provisions relating to postal voting and voting by proxy have now been extended to parish council elections.[4]

Detailed rules for nomination of candidates and the conduct of an election of parish councillors will be found in the rules made by the Secretary of State referred to above, and also the forms for use thereat and the form of declaration of acceptance of office by the chairman of a parish council, and by a parish councillor. (*See* "Chairman of Parish Council" and "Parish Councillor".)

The Representation of the People Acts contain provisions relating to corrupt and illegal practices and the control of election expenses of candidates. There is a limit on

---

[1] R.P.A. 1983, s. 37.
[2] R.P.A. 1983, s. 35(1).
[3] R.P.A. 1983, s. 35(4).
[4] R.P.A. 1985, s. 28 and Sch. 5.

expenses which is increased from time to time by Statutory Instrument. Every candidate must make a return of expenses, accompanied by a declaration in the form prescribed by the Secretary of State; this must be sent to the clerk of the district council within 28 days after the date of the election.

A candidate at an election is entitled, for the purpose of holding public meetings in furtherance of his candidature, to the use, free of charge, at reasonable times between the last day on which notice of the election may be published and the day preceding the day of election, of a suitable room in the premises of a community, foundation or voluntary school situated in the electoral area for which he is a candidate (or if there is no such school in that area, in any such school in an adjacent electoral area), or in a parish or community in part comprised in that electoral area.

He may also use any meeting room situated in the electoral area for which he is standing or in a parish or community in part comprised in that electoral area, the expense of maintaining which is payable wholly or mainly out of public funds or out of any rate, or by a body whose expenses are so payable. The school hours must not be interfered with; nor may any part of the school premises which is used as part of a private dwelling-house be used for the above purpose. Furthermore, the candidate must defray any expense incurred by reason of the use of the room for the purpose of his candidature and the cost of making good any damage caused by such use.[1]

The district or unitary council shall pay the expenses properly incurred in holding the election, not exceeding such scale as may be fixed so far as applicable. Where polls for the election of parish councillors and district or

---

[1] R.P.A. 1983, s. 96, as substituted by R.P.A. 1985, Sch. 4, para. 38.

unitary councillors for the same area are taken together, one-half of the expenses is to be treated as attributable to the election of parish councillors. However, the district or unitary council may require the parish or community council to repay the election expenses it incurs.[1]

If a parish council has not been properly constituted, or becomes unable to act from failure to elect or otherwise, the district or unitary council may order a new election to be held and may, by order, make provision for authorising any person to act temporarily in the place of the parish council and of the chairman of the parish council. They are empowered for the above purpose to do anything which is deemed necessary or expedient for carrying the order into effect.[2]

In the event of a casual vacancy upon a parish council by death or disqualification or in any other way, the vacancy must be publicly notified and a by-election conducted in accordance with the rules for ordinary elections if within 14 days a poll is claimed by ten electors.[3] Otherwise, it is to be filled by co-option as soon as practicable and the council must be convened forthwith to fill the vacancy if the period of vacancy has six months or more to run. If the period is less than six months, the council may still fill the vacancy by co-option if it so chooses but it is not obliged to do so.[4] The person filling a casual vacancy retires from office at the time when the councillor whose place he has filled would ordinarily have retired.[5]

---

[1] R.P.A. 1983, s. 36(5), as amended by the Local Government Finance (Repeals and Consequential Amendments) Order 1991.

[2] R.P.A. 1983, s. 39(4).

[3] Local Elections (Parishes and Communities) (England and Wales) Rules 2006 (S.I. 3305).

[4] L.G.A. 1972, s. 89(6), and Local Elections (Parishes and Communities) (England and Wales) Rules 2006 (S.I. 3305), rule 5.

[5] L.G.A. 1972, s. 90.

If there is more than one candidate for co-option, the council must vote, if necessary by successive counts which eliminate the least successful candidate, until the successful candidate receives an *absolute* majority of those present at the council meeting and voting.

If the membership of a parish council has been increased during the term of office of the existing members, the vacancies are not casual and must be filled by a by-election.

### Appointment

Section 16A of the Local Government Act 1972 (added by section 76 of the Local Government and Public Involvement in Health Act 2007) empowers a parish council in England to appoint persons to the council in accordance with regulations made by the Secretary of State. No regulations have so far been made.

## ELECTORS

**(See Local Government Electors)**

## ELIGIBILITY FOR OFFICE

**(See Parish Councillor)**

## EMPLOYEES

**(See *also* Agency—Clerk of Parish Council—Deputy Officers—Gratuities to Officers—Superannuation of Paid Officers—Treasurer of Parish Council)**

A parish council has a general power to employ any persons it considers necessary for the proper discharge of its functions.[1] If the function is one which the parish council does not have a specific statutory power to perform but is covered by the free resource or by the power of the promotion of well-being, the cost must be borne by one or other of these funds[2] (*see* "Free Resource" and "Promotion of Well-Being"). An example is the employment of a village sweeper. Every appointment of a paid officer or employee must be made on merit.[3]

In the case of any paid employee, including the clerk, the council has certain obligations. These include the deduction and payment to HM Revenue and Customs of income tax and the payment of National Insurance contributions as appropriate.

Fidelity security is essential (*see* "Insurance").

All employees have extensive rights under employment rights legislation, including the right to be provided with a written statement of the employer's terms and conditions of service.[4]

All employees in Wales are subject to a code of conduct issued by the National Assembly.[5] The code came into force on 28th July 2001. The Secretary of State in England has power to promote such a code. At the date of publication of this book, no code had been published.

Care must be taken to comply with the statutory obligations to ensure the health and safety of employees.[6]

---

[1]  L.G.A. 1972, s. 112.
[2]  L.G.A. 1972, s. 137; L.G.A. 2000, s. 2.
[3]  L.G.H.A. 1989, s. 7.
[4]  Employment Rights Act 1996, s. 1.
[5]  Code of Conduct (Qualifying Local Government Employees) (Wales) Order 2001 (S.I. 2280 (W.170)).
[6]  Health and Safety at Work etc. Act 1974.

Insurance in respect of the council's liability against injury sustained by an employee during the course of his employment is *compulsory*, whether the employee is part-time or full-time.[1]

Any council faced with a claim for unfair dismissal or sex, race or disability discrimination should seek legal advice, as each case tends to turn on its own facts and the financial consequences to the council may be considerable.

## ENTERTAINMENT AND THE ARTS

### (See *also* Tourism)

A parish council has the power to provide entertainments of any nature or facilities for dancing.[2] It can provide a theatre, a concert hall, a dance hall or any other premises suitable for entertainments. It can spend money on maintaining a band or orchestra. It may do anything which furthers the development of the arts and local crafts. A parish council may set apart any part of its parks or pleasure grounds for any of these purposes subject to any covenant. It can also contribute to the expenses of any other local authority or anyone who is providing any of these facilities.

## EXPENSES AND EXPENDITURE

### (See *also* Allowances to Parish Councillors—Loans to Parish Council)

A parish council is empowered to incur expenditure in the execution of any works, including works of maintenance or improvement, or on anything which is calculated to

---

[1] Employer's Liability (Compulsory Insurance) Act 1969.
[2] L.G.A. 1972, s. 145.

facilitate, or is conducive or incidental to, the exercise of its statutory powers[1] (all of which are indicated under their appropriate headings in this book) or in relation to any parish property. There is also a power to incur expenditure for the benefit of the area for all or some of its inhabitants.[2] (*See* "Free Resource".) Since the beginning of 2009, "eligible" parish councils in England have also been able to incur expenditure on the promotion of well-being for their inhabitants. (*See* "Promotion of Well-Being".)

With the exception of expenditure under the "free resource", all rate limits have now been abolished.[3]

The expenses of a parish council are chargeable separately on the parish and the council obtains funds for the purpose of defraying these expenses by means of precepts issued to the council responsible for collecting local government taxes.[4] A parish council is a local precepting authority and may issue a precept for each financial year before 1st March in the preceding financial year (although it is not invalid merely because it is issued on or after that date).[5] It is important for councils to prepare accurate budgets in order to ensure that they will receive the monies during the year which are necessary for the proper carrying out of the council's functions. The council responsible for the collection of local government taxes cannot challenge the amount of the precept. It is inadvisable for a parish council to make any arrangement with that council which interferes with its right to precept. If there is a separate council, the expenses of the parish meeting are paid by the parish council. These expenses will form part of the

---

[1] L.G.A. 1972, s. 111.
[2] L.G.A. 1972, s. 137.
[3] *ibid.*
[4] i.e. the district or unitary council. L.G.A. 1972, s. 150.
[5] L.G.F.A. 1992, s. 41.

ordinary expenses of the parish council.

The expenses of a district or unitary council are normally charged as general expenses on the whole of the district or county but a district or unitary council must charge as special expenses on a parish any expenses incurred in the parish by performing therein any function performed elsewhere in the district or county by a parish council, unless it passes a resolution to treat them as general expenses.[1]

Every cheque or other order for payment of money by a parish council must be signed by two members of the council. (*See* "Accounts".) This is a responsible duty and every signatory must ensure that payments are made only in accordance with the decisions of the council.

Where there is no parish council, a parish meeting in England meets its own expenses, usually by precepting on the district or unitary council. In Wales, the expenses of a community meeting where there is no community council are met by the county or county borough council.

For the tax position of parish councils, *see* "Income Tax" and "Value Added Tax".

## FIDELITY SECURITY

### (See Insurance—Treasurer of Parish Council)

## FIELD GARDENS

### (See Allotments)

---

[1]   L.G.F.A. 1992, s. 35.

# FINANCE

**(See Accounts—Allowances to Parish Councillors—
Audit—Expenses and Expenditure—Free Resource—
Funds and Accumulations—Income Tax—Investment
—Loans to Parish Council—Rating and Valuation—
Subscriptions to Associations—Value Added Tax)**

# FINANCIAL STATEMENT OF PARISH COUNCIL

**(See Accounts—Audit)**

# FLAGPOLES

A parish council may with the consent of the highway authority erect flagpoles on any highway in its own area and may make slots in the highway for them.

The parish council must ensure that the apparatus causes as little obstruction to the highway or interference with the enjoyment of adjacent premises as possible, does not interfere with traffic signs, and is properly maintained and (if necessary to prevent danger) lit.[1]

# FLYPOSTING

**(See Graffiti and Flyposting)**

# FOOTPATHS

**(See *also* Footways—Highways)**

A public footpath is a highway over which the public have

---

[1] H.A. 1980, s. 144.

a right of way on foot only, other than a path at the side of a public road.[1] The latter are usually known as footways. (*See* "Footways".) A public bridleway is a footpath with additional rights, i.e. to ride or lead a horse.

A parish council may create a public footpath (or any highway) by means of an agreement with the landowner.[2] In addition, the parish council may undertake the repair and maintenance of all or any of the public footpaths or bridleways within its parish. The exercise of this power will not relieve any other authority or person from any liability with respect to repair or maintenance of a public footpath. In particular, the county council must maintain all paths in existence in December 1949.[3] For the *standard* of repair, *see* "Highways". It is entirely optional whether a parish council undertakes the repair of any public footpath. It cannot be compelled to do so. If the parish council resolves to repair, it should inform the county council, as the highway authority in all parishes. The county council may in such cases meet the whole or part of the expenditure incurred by the parish council.

For obstruction of footpaths generally, *see* "Highways". A parish council has no power to compel an owner to cut back hedges but the county council or district council may so order the owner to do this at the request of the parish council if it is necessary to keep the footpaths safe and fit for normal use.[4]

A landowner has a legal duty to keep gates and stiles safe and to the standard of repair necessary to prevent unreasonable interference with users, but the landowner

[1]   H.A. 1980, s. 30.
[2]   H.A. 1980, s. 43.
[3]   H.A. 1980, s. 36.
[4]   H.A. 1980, s. 154.

may claim a quarter of his expenses from the highway authority. If he fails in his duty, the highway authority may do the work at his expense after 14 days' notice.[1]

Driving a motor vehicle or riding a motor-cycle on a footpath or bridleway is an offence. However, restrictions on the use of vehicles on footpaths, footways or bridleways do not affect the use by the parish council of vehicles or equipment for the maintenance of the way within certain prescribed limits.[2] It is not a criminal offence to ride a horse on a footpath (although it is on a footway), unless there is a by-law in force to this effect.

There is no obligation on a parish council to fence a footpath or to maintain an existing fence. If, however, the council removes and fails to replace a fence erected by it or its predecessors to guard a dangerous place, the council may be liable under the law of tort in respect of any accident resulting therefrom.

Where a public path crosses agricultural land, or land which is being brought into use for agriculture, and it is convenient and in accordance with the rules of good husbandry to plough the path in ploughing the land, the farmer may do so. This does not, however, apply to a path at the side of a field. After the ploughing is completed, if the disturbance to the surface is for sowing a crop, he must make good the surface of the path for the exercise of the public right of way not later than two weeks from the time when he *began* to plough the path. This period may be extended, on application, for a further period not exceeding 28 days. Failure to restore within the time limits renders him liable to a fine at level 3 on the standard scale

[1]   H.A. 1980, s. 146.
[2]   R.T.A. 1988, s. 34; H.A. 1980, s. 300.

for summary offences (currently £1,000).[1] A farmer who ploughs any path otherwise than in exercise of the above right to plough is guilty of an offence and subject to a fine at level 3 on the standard scale (currently £1,000). A prosecution can be brought by the highway authority or by the parish council.

The Highways Act 1980 has been further amended in respect of disturbance to footpaths and bridleways by the Rights of Way Act 1990.

If it is represented to the highway authority that for agricultural purposes it is expedient that stiles, gates or other works for preventing the ingress or egress of animals should be erected on a public footpath crossing the land, the highway authority may authorise their erection subject to such conditions as they may impose for maintenance and for enabling the right of way to be exercised without undue inconvenience to the public.[2]

A parish council has power to erect direction posts on public paths with the consent of the county council. Such posts may also be erected by the county council, as highway authority. The county council has a *duty* to erect signposts at every point where a footpath or bridleway or a byway open to all traffic leaves a metalled road, unless the parish council agrees with the county council that a sign is not necessary.[3] Parish councils should ensure that the county councils comply with this statutory duty.

It is an offence on or near any way shown on the definitive map to put a notice containing any false or misleading

---

[1] H.A. 1980, s. 134, as amended and substituted by the Rights of Way Act 1990.

[2] H.A. 1980, s. 147.

[3] C.A. 1968, s. 27, as amended by the Wildlife and Countryside Act 1981, s. 65.

statement likely to deter the public from using the way.[1] It is the duty of the highway authority to enforce this provision, and they or the district or unitary council[2] can bring proceedings for this purpose.

It is unlawful for a bull to be at large in a field through which there is a footpath unless it does not exceed the age of ten months or, not being of a recognised dairy breed, it is at large with cows or heifers in the same field.[3] A recognised dairy breed means one of the following: Ayrshire, British Friesian, British Holstein, Dairy Shorthorn, Guernsey, Jersey or Kerry.

Any question of the improper use of the highway, e.g. the use of a footpath by cycles or other vehicles, is not directly a matter for the parish council but for the highway authority. As a result of the Countryside Act 1968, a cycle may legally be ridden on a bridleway.[4]

The use of a footpath includes the use of prams and push-chairs as a reasonable accompaniment of a pedestrian.[5] It has never been decided by the courts whether a dog is a reasonable accompaniment of a pedestrian, although it is usually assumed that this is so. However, just like the pedestrian, if the dog strays from the footpath, there is technically a trespass. In practice this can only be avoided by keeping the dog on a lead.

## FOOTWAYS

A footway is a footpath at the side of a public road. It is part of the highway and is maintainable by the highway

---

[1] N.P.A. 1949, s. 57.
[2] L.G.A. 1972, Sch. 21, para. 97.
[3] Wildlife and Countryside Act 1981, s. 59.
[4] C.A. 1968, s. 30.
[5] *R. v. Mathias* (1861) 2 F. & F. 570.

authority. A highway authority has a duty to provide a footway in any case where it considers that the provision of such a footway is necessary or desirable for the safety or accommodation of pedestrians.[1]

The law relating to footpaths (*see* "Footpaths") does not, in general terms, apply to footways. Thus, a parish council has no specific power to maintain a footway.

A parish council may provide seats and shelters on a footway (*see* "Roadside Seats and Shelters" and "Bus Shelters"). For footway lighting, *see* "Lighting".

# FREE RESOURCE

## (*See also* Promotion of Well-Being)

The Local Government (Financial Provisions) Act 1963 first gave parish councils this very useful general power in what came to be known as the free fifth. Subsequently, it was extended by the 1972 Act into the free twopence and, following changes in the rating system, it is now usual to refer to it as the "free resource".[2] Under it, a parish council may spend every year up to a specified limit on anything which in the opinion of the parish council is in the interests of the parish, or any part of it, or is in the interests of all or some of its inhabitants. Examples include Armistice Day wreaths, employment of village sweeper, presentation to retiring member, etc. It may also be used to make contributions to any charitable body or any body providing a public service otherwise than for gain, anywhere

---

[1] H.A. 1980, s. 54.

[2] L.G.A. 1972, s. 137, as amended. The amount is currently £6.15 per elector on the electoral roll on 1st April in both England and Wales. Under the Local Government Act 2003, the amount can be increased in line with the movement of retail prices.

in the United Kingdom, or to any appeal fund devised in connection with a particular event in the United Kingdom by the Lord Mayor of London or the Chairman of a county or district council. For the use of the free resource in connection with land acquired for the benefit of the area, *see* "Property of Parish Council".

These terms are very wide and the reference to "the council's opinion" ensures that, provided the council do not act quite unreasonably, their discretion is not open to challenge.

The power is, however, subject to the limitation that it may not be used where some other power, whether conditional or unconditional, is available. This means that the power cannot be used to circumvent a requirement for Ministerial consent, or to evade some restriction on the amount which can be spent for a certain purpose.

It is important that the expenditure be authorised in advance by a formal resolution of the council. This is because such expenditure should be shown in a separate account, which is to be open to inspection by a local government elector in the same way as are the council's accounts (*see* "Inspection of Documents").

## FREEDOM OF INFORMATION

Under the Freedom of Information Act 2000, all local authorities, including parish councils, and parish meetings in England where there is no council, must make available to the public certain types of information. In particular, they must adopt and maintain a publication scheme showing the information they provide and how it can be inspected.[1] Each scheme must be approved by

---

[1] Freedom of Information Act 2000, s. 19.

the Information Commissioner, who may issue model schemes.[1] Model schemes for local councils, and parish meetings where there is no council, have been published and can be viewed on the Commissioner's website (www. informationcommissioner.gov.uk).

Most of the information required to be published under the 2000 Act is already covered by other legislation (see "Inspection of Documents").

# FUEL ALLOTMENTS

**(See Allotments)**

# FUND RAISING

**(See Income)**

# FUNDS AND ACCUMULATIONS

A parish council has power to set up a loans fund for debt repayment,[2] and such other funds, other than a superannuation fund, as it thinks fit.[3] It may pay into such funds such sums as it thinks fit. Thus a parish council may provide for the renewal and repair of any of its assets. In respect of the application of capital money on disposal of land, the consent of the Secretary of State is required under section 153 of the Local Government Act 1972. A general disposal consent has been issued by him – Communities and Local Government Circular 06/03: *general disposal consent (England) 2003*. The Welsh Assembly has issued

---

[1] Freedom of Information Act 2000, s. 20.

[2] L.G.A. 1972, Sch. 13 – funds of local authorities, para. 15.

[3] L.G.(M.P.)A. 1976, s. 28.

its own circular – National Assembly for Wales Circular 2003: *Local Government Act 1972: general disposal consent (Wales) 2003*.

Pending the application of the funds for their respective purposes, the money in the fund should be invested. (*See* "Investment".)

## GIFTS OF PROPERTY

**(See Bus Shelters—Property of Parish Council—War Memorials)**

## GRAFFITI AND FLYPOSTING

A parish council has power to issue fixed penalty notices for defacement caused by graffiti and flyposting. The Secretary of State has power to prescribe conditions to be applied to a parish council in relation to the authorisation of persons to give fixed penalty notices.[1]

## GRANTS

A parish council may be able to obtain a grant from several sources. A county council may make a grant to a parish council, or a parish meeting in England without a council, towards expenditure relating to public open spaces.[2] Fields in Trust (formerly the National Playing Fields Association), Ground Floor South, 100 Christian Street, London E1 1RS (www.fieldsintrust.org.uk) may provide a grant for the provision of playing fields and equipment. Grants for sports provision may also be available from, or through, Sport

---

[1] A.S.B.A. 2003, ss. 43, 43B and 47.
[2] L.G.A. 1958, s. 56.

England, 3rd Floor, Victoria House, Bloomsbury Square, London WC1B 4SE or the Sports Council for Wales, Sophia Gardens, Cardiff CF1 9SW. Natural England, 1 East Parade, Sheffield S1 2ET has power to grant-aid expenditure for the conservation and enhancement of the natural beauty and amenity of the countryside or for the provision of facilities for the enjoyment of the countryside.[1] D.E.F.R.A. may give grants for broadly the same purposes under the Countryside Stewardship scheme.[2] A highway authority or a district council may contribute to expenditure by a parish council on footpath or bridleway maintenance.[3]

The Secretary of State may grant-aid any body which encourages the public not to deface places by litter and a county council or a district council may contribute towards the provision by a parish council of litter bins.[4] The Secretary of State may give grants for the reclaiming or improvement of derelict land.[5] A.C.R.E. (Action for Communities in Rural England), Somerford Court, Somerford Road, Cirencester, Glos. GL7 1TW administers grant funds for village halls and for rural improvement projects in England. In Wales, grants may be available for environmental projects from the Countryside Council for Wales, Maes y Ffynnon, Penrhosgarnedd, Bangor, Gwynedd LL57 2DN. Parish councils may be able to obtain grants from the National Heritage Memorial Fund and the other National Lottery funds. Some principal councils make concurrent function grants to parish councils to cover the whole, or part, of the expenditure by a parish council on a concurrent function which is exercised by the principal council as well.

---

[1] Natural Environment and Rural Communities Act 2006, s. 6.
[2] Environment Act 1998, s. 98.
[3] H.A. 1980, s. 43(2).
[4] Litter Act 1983, ss. 3 and 6.
[5] Derelict Land Act 1982, s. 1.

## GRATUITIES TO OFFICERS

The general effect of case law is that remuneration must be related to the current responsibilities of the office and any gratuity not so related is ordinarily illegal.

Gratuities may, however, be payable upon retirement; *see* "Superannuation of Paid Officers".

## GRAVES

### (See Burial and Cremation)

## GREENS

### (See Village Greens)

## GROUPING OF PARISHES

### England

A parish may be grouped under an order of the district, unitary or London borough council with some neighbouring (not necessarily adjoining) parish or parishes under a common parish council.[1] In such cases, however, there must be a separate parish meeting for every parish so grouped. Each parish must be separately represented on the parish council for the group. The grouping may be dissolved upon application to the principal council by the council of the grouped parishes or of the parish meeting for any one of the grouped parishes.

---

[1] L.G.A. 1972, ss. 11 and 29. Note: s. 11 of the L.G.A. 1972 has been amended to include London borough councils since they now have powers to carry out community governance reviews (*see* "Alteration of Areas").

The parish meeting of any parish may apply to the principal council for a voluntary grouping order. The consent of the parish meetings of the other parishes proposed to be grouped is essential.

Where a grouping order is in force, it provides for preserving the separate rights of each parish as to appointments of trustees and beneficiaries of charities and the custody of documents, and may provide for the consent of a particular parish meeting to any particular act of the council.

The rule that, in England, the number of councillors on a parish council must not be less than five[1] does not mean that there must be at least five councillors for each parish in the group. The number from each parish can be less.

A group may adopt an alternative style and be known as a group of "communities", "neighbourhoods" or "villages". (*See* "Name and Style of Parish".)

**Wales**

A community meeting may apply to the county or county borough council for an order grouping the community with some neighbouring community or communities under a common community council, or for adding the community to an existing common community council. However, an application may only be made if (a) a poll of local government electors for the community has been held, (b) a majority of those voting in the poll supports the application, and (c) the application is made jointly with the communities to be grouped. The decision to hold a poll must be made at a community meeting at which at least 30% of the electorate or, if that number exceeds 300, at least 300, electors are present. At least 30 clear days' notice of the meeting must be given.

---

[1] L.G.A. 1972, s. 16(1).

A similar procedure applies where the dissolution of a common community council is sought.

If a proposal to form or dissolve a common community council is rejected in a poll, a further poll cannot be held for at least two years. Furthermore, such a proposal cannot be made for two years after changes made following a review by the Local Government Boundary Commission for Wales or following a successful application for a grouping/dissolution order.[1]

## GUARANTEE POLICY

### (See Insurance—Treasurer of Parish Council)

## HACKNEY CARRIAGE

### (See Licences)

## HALLS

### (See Village Halls)

## HERBAGE

### (See Roadside Wastes)

## HIGHWAYS

### (See also Flagpoles—Footpaths—Roadside Wastes)

The county council, metropolitan district council or unitary council (in Wales, the county or county borough council)

---

[1] L.G.A. 1972, ss. 28-30.

is the local highway authority for all highways in a parish, although the district council may have certain powers.[1]

The word "highway" includes all defined routes (e.g. roads, bridges, carriageways, cartways, horseways, footpaths, bridleways, footways, causeways, churchways and pavements) over which members of the public may lawfully pass. The highway authority will be responsible for the maintenance of most of these to the standard required by law, i.e. to be reasonably passable for the ordinary traffic of the neighbourhood for all seasons of the year.[2] The duty to repair can be enforced if necessary by following the procedure laid down in the Highways Act 1980.[3]

## Is there a right of way?

Where a way over any land has been actually enjoyed by the public as of right and without interruption for 20 years, it shall be deemed to have been dedicated as a highway, unless there is sufficient evidence that there was no intention during that period to dedicate.[4] A right of way over land does not include a public right of navigation over a river.[5]

An owner of land (or the reversioner, where the land is let or leased) over which a way used by the public passes may place a notice on the land indicating that the way is not dedicated as a highway. Any such notice, placed in such a manner as to be visible to those using the way, shall, in the absence of proof of a contrary intention, be sufficient evidence to negate the intention of the owner to dedicate the way as a highway.[6]

---

[1]  H.A. 1980, s. 1(2).
[2]  *R. v. High Halden* (1859) 1 F. & F. 678.
[3]  H.A. 1980, s. 56.
[4]  H.A. 1980, s. 31. *Gloucestershire C.C. v. Farrow* (1983) 2 All E.R. 1031.
[5]  *Yorkshire Derwent Trust Ltd. v. Brotherton* [1989] 2 All E.R. 423.
[6]  H.A. 1980, s. 31(3).

However, if no such notice has been displayed, or if it has been torn down or defaced, notice in writing sent by the owner of the land to the council of the county and to the council of the district in which the way is situate stating that the way is not dedicated, shall, in the absence of proof of a contrary intention, be sufficient evidence to negate the intention of the owner to dedicate the way as a highway.[1]

The owner of any land may deposit at any time with the council of the county and with the council of the district in which the land is situate, a map on a scale of not less than six inches to the mile, delineating his land, together with a statement indicating what ways he admits have been dedicated as highways.[2]

The Act does not require these maps and statements to be deposited with parish councils, but parish councils should, nevertheless, take steps to inspect them, so that they may be in a position to make representations to the district council regarding any public rights of way not shown on any such maps or indicated in the statement accompanying the map.

Any court or other tribunal, before determining whether a way has been dedicated as a highway, or the date upon which dedication, if any, took place, shall take into consideration "any map, plan or history of the locality, or other relevant document tendered in evidence", and that such weight shall be given thereto as the court or tribunal considers justified by the circumstances.

**Definitive maps and statements**

Most rights of way in England and Wales are shown on maps prepared and kept up to date by surveying authorities

---

[1] H.A. 1980, s. 31(5).
[2] H.A. 1980, s. 31(6).

(county councils, metropolitan district councils, London borough councils and unitary councils in England; county and county borough councils in Wales). Depiction of a path or way on the definitive map is conclusive evidence that there is a public right of way. There is a fairly elaborate procedure for altering the definitive map where a change in the path network takes place. Parish councils have a right to be consulted about, and to be notified of, any proposed changes.

The definitive map is accompanied by a definitive statement. This describes the route of each path and any limitations or conditions, both legal and physical, to which the path may be subject. In practice, most definitive statements simply describe briefly the route of a path.

The principal legislation covering definitive maps is the National Parks and Access to the Countryside Act 1949 and the Wildlife and Countryside Act 1981.

### Acquisition and agreements

Where the parish council is satisfied that the dedication of a highway will be for the benefit of the inhabitants of the parish, or of any part thereof, it may enter into an agreement with any person having the necessary power for the dedication by that person of a highway over land in the parish or any adjoining parish.[1] Any right of way so acquired would necessarily be a public highway dedicated to general public use.

A parish council may also acquire by agreement a right of way which is *not* a public highway, e.g. one restricted to the inhabitants of the parish or any part thereof.[2]

---

[1] H.A. 1980, s. 30.
[2] L.G.A. 1894, s. 8.

The parish council may carry out any maintenance or improvement work to any such highway or right of way. It may be noted that the above powers are not limited to footpaths, but include carriageways.

The district council, with the consent of the highway authority and the local planning authority, may also acquire rights of way both by agreement and compulsorily.

## Obstructions

If a parish council considers that any highway has been unlawfully stopped up or obstructed, it may make representation to that effect to the county council which then has a *duty* to take proceedings to remove the obstruction, unless satisfied that the allegations are incorrect.[1] The fact that the highway is not on the definitive map does not preclude the county council from taking action if there is clear evidence of the existence of the public right of way.[2]

The special needs of disabled or blind persons in respect of obstacles on the highway must be considered by the highway authority.[3]

(For encroachment on roadside wastes forming part of the highway – *see* "Roadside Wastes".)

## Provision of trees and verges

The parish council may, with the consent of the highway authority, plant trees, shrubs and other plants and lay out grass verges in a highway maintainable at the public expense.[4] This power includes a power to do anything

---

[1] H.A. 1980, s. 130.
[2] *R. v. Ogden* [1963] 1 All E.R. 574.
[3] H.A. 1980, s. 175A.
[4] H.A. 1980, s. 116.

expedient for the maintenance or protection of anything provided by them or anyone else, including the provision (and subsequent removal) of guards or fences to protect the plantings. As a result of private Acts, parish councils in some counties may carry out such work without the consent of the highway authority.

## Stopping up, or diversion, of a highway or public path

In the case of a highway other than a trunk or special road, a highway authority may apply to the magistrates' court for authority to stop it up or divert it on the ground that is unnecessary[1] or that a diversion will make it nearer or more commodious to the public.[2] If the highway is a classified road, the parish council or, in England if none, the chairman of the parish meeting must, amongst others, be given at least 28 days' notice and is entitled to appear before the magistrates' court and be heard. Any other person likely to be aggrieved may also be heard and this presumably includes a parish council of a neighbouring parish. If, however, the highway is an unclassified road, the highway authority must give notice that it proposes to make the application to both the district council and the parish council or, in England where there is no parish council, to the Chairman of the parish meeting, and if within two months any of these give notice to the highway authority that they have refused their consent, the highway authority may not make the application at all.

Any two magistrates of the court may view the highway in question. The court cannot authorise a diversion without the written consent of all those with legal interests in the land over which the diversion is to be made, and an order can reserve a footway or bridleway.

---

[1] For the meaning of unnecessary see *Ramblers Association v. Kent* C.C. [1990] 60 Planning and Compensation Reports, 464.

[2] H.A. 1980, s. 96.

Whilst the magistrates' court procedure is only available to highway authorities and applies, apart from trunk and special roads, to all highways including footpaths and bridleways, a county council or a district council has a special procedure available to it for extinguishing by order a public right of way over any footpath or bridleway in its area.[1] The council can make such an order (called a public path extinguishment order) *only on the ground that the path or way is not needed for public use.* If the order is opposed, it must be confirmed by the Secretary of State and, before it is submitted to him for confirmation, the council must give at least 28 days' notice in the *London Gazette*, a local newspaper and to the parish council or parish meeting, and must post a notice near the land concerned. If objections are made, the Secretary of State holds a public inquiry. He is bound to hold such an inquiry if the objector is a local authority (including a parish council, or parish meeting if there is no parish council). If the order is not opposed, the district council may confirm the order themselves.

A council (a county council or a local authority) has power to make an order – known as a special extinguishment order – stopping up or diverting a "relevant highway" (a) for the purpose of preventing or reducing crime which would otherwise disrupt the life of the community, or (b) which crosses school premises, to protect pupils and staff from violence or the threat of violence, harassment, alarm or distress arising from unlawful authority, or any other risk to health or safety from such activity. A "relevant highway" is a footpath, bridleway, restricted byway, road used as a public path or byway open to all traffic.[2]

The proprietor of a school may apply to a council (defined above) for a special extinguishment or diversion order for a

---

[1] H.A. 1980, s. 118; Public Path Orders Regulations 1993 (S.I. 11).
[2] H.A. 1980, ss. 118B and 119B.

relevant highway (*see above*) which crosses school premises. The proprietor is the person or body of persons responsible for the management and, for a community, foundation or voluntary school, a community or foundation special school or a maintained nursery school, this means the governing body.[1]

A county council or district council also has a power to make a similar order for diversion of a footpath or bridleway (called a public path diversion order), where it appears to the council that, in the interests of the owner or occupier of the land crossed by the path or way, it is expedient to divert it.[2] There is provision in respect of confirmation by the Secretary of State if the order is opposed, with the important provision that the Secretary of State must then be satisfied that the diverted path will not be substantially less convenient to the public.

A council (county council and local authority) may make a gating order by which a physical barrier to restrict public access is placed across a highway. A gating order may be made where the council is satisfied that anti-social or criminal activities are affecting premises adjoining the highway. It is expected that the power will be exercised, if at all, to close paths and alleys which run behind and between properties and which are alleged to facilitate criminal behaviour. Closure may be at all times or only at certain times of the day. Motorways, trunk roads and classified or principal roads are excluded from the power to make gating orders.[3]

---

[1] H.A. 1980, ss. 118C and 119C.

[2] H.A. 1980, s. 119, as amended by the Wildlife and Countryside Act 1981, Sch. 16, para. 5. See also the Public Path Orders Regulations 1993 (S.I. 9).

[3] H.A. 1980, ss. 129A-129G.

Other provisions relating to stopping up or diverting highways are as follows. A housing authority may extinguish rights of way over land purchased for slum clearance and redevelopment. Similar provision is made for the extinguishment of public rights of way over land acquired or appropriated for planning purposes by a local authority if that authority is satisfied that an alternative right of way has been or will be provided, or is not required in the circumstances.

The Acquisition of Land Act 1981 confers a general power if land is purchased, whether compulsorily or by agreement where a power of compulsory acquisition could have been used, to stop up public rights of way other than those enjoyed by vehicular traffic, subject to the Secretary of State being satisfied that an alternative right of way has been or will be provided, or is not required in the circumstances.[1]

There is also a provision in the Town and Country Planning Act 1990 for the stopping up or diversion of highways (including footpaths or bridleways) by order of the Secretary of State if he is satisfied that it is necessary to do so in order to enable development to be carried out in accordance with a planning permission, or in certain other circumstances.[2] The county council, or district council exercising planning powers, now has similar powers, subject to confirmation by the Secretary of State.[3]

The Secretary of State may, in connection with the construction or improvement of a highway, make an order diverting or stopping up any other highway if it appears to him to be expedient to do so, in the interests of the safety

---

[1] Acquisition of Land Act 1981, s. 32.
[2] T.C.P.A. 1990, s. 247.
[3] T.C.P.A. 1990, s. 259; Town and Country Planning (Public Path Orders) Regulations 1993 (S.I. 10).

of users of the main highway or to facilitate the movement of traffic on the main highway.

A highway over which the public has a right of way with vehicles (not being a trunk road or other main road) may be converted by Ministerial Order to a footpath or bridleway if a resolution by the local planning authority for improving the amenity of their area includes a proposal to convert a highway in that manner.

### Signs

A parish council may put up a village name sign,[1] a bus stop, or a warning sign on a public highway, other than a footpath or bridleway, with the permission of the local highway authority. It may also provide warning signs on footpaths or bridleways without such permission.[2] (For direction signs on footpaths, *see* "Footpaths.")

### Control of roadside sales

Sales from stalls on vehicles which are stationed either on a verge or a layby or on any unenclosed land within 15 metres of the road are unlawful if their presence causes, or is likely to cause, danger on the road or interrupts, or is likely to interrupt, any user of the road.[3]

### Traffic calming

A parish council may contribute towards the cost of traffic calming measures (e.g. road humps) provided by a highway authority if the council thinks they will be of benefit to its area.[4]

---

[1] Which may include a crest, with the Secretary of State's permission.
[2] R.T.R.A. 1984, s. 72.
[3] H.A. 1980, s. 147A, inserted by L.G.(M.P.)A. 1982, s. 23.
[4] H.A. 1980, s. 274A, inserted by L.G.R.A. 1997, s. 30.

## HIRING OF LAND

**(See Allotments—Property of Parish Council)**

## HOUSE TO HOUSE COLLECTIONS

**(See Income)**

## HOUSING

Parish councils have no statutory functions in regard to the provision of housing. There seems no reason, however, why a parish council should not acquire land by agreement to make this available for a housing association if in the council's opinion this would be for the benefit of the parish.[1]

A parish council may complain to the officer of the council responsible for public health in writing that any house is unfit for human habitation or that any area should be dealt with as a clearance area, whereupon that officer has a duty to inspect the house or the area and to report to the housing authority stating the facts and whether, in his opinion, the house is unfit or the area should be so treated.[2]

## INCLOSURE OF COMMONS

**(See Commons)**

## INCOME

**(See *also* Expenses—Lotteries)**

A parish council obtains most of its income for its own

---

[1] L.G.A. 1972, s. 124.
[2] Housing Act 1985, s. 606(2), as amended.

revenue purposes through precepts to the council responsible for the collection of local government taxes,[1] but may also have, or utilise, a number of other sources, e.g. income from letting property; income from investments and bank deposits; income from public subscriptions, whist drives, etc. House to house collections require a licence from the council responsible for the collection of local government taxes, unless the purpose of the collection is purely local in character and a certificate of exemption is obtained from the Chief Constable.[2]

## INCOME TAX

### (See *also* Value Added Tax)

Parish councils are not liable for income tax on their income, nor for corporation tax or capital gains tax.[3]

## INCORPORATION OF PARISH COUNCIL

### (See Parish Council)

## INFORMATION ABOUT LAND

A parish council requiring information about the ownership or occupation of land with a view to exercising any of its statutory functions may serve a notice on the occupier, freeholder, leaseholder, mortgagee, any person receiving rent, or any person authorised to manage or let the land. The notice must specify the land and the statutory function and may require the person served to advise the council of

---

[1] L.G.F.A. 1992, s. 41.
[2] House to House Collections Act 1939, s. 1.
[3] Income and Corporation Taxes Act 1988, s. 519 and Taxation of Chargeable Gains Act 1992, s. 271.

the nature of his own interest and the name and address of the occupier and every person believed by him to fall into one of the above categories.[1]

If the land has registered title, this procedure may not be necessary because the Register is open to public inspection.

## INFORMATION FOR THE PUBLIC

### (*See also* Freedom of Information)

A parish council may make arrangements, or assist in the making of arrangements, whereby the public may readily obtain on application information on services provided by *any* local authority, government department, charity or voluntary organisation, or any other information relating to the functions of the parish council.[2] A parish council may, in connection with the provision of information on the functions of the parish council, arrange for publications, lectures, films, exhibitions, etc., or contribute towards the cost of preparing these.

## INQUIRIES

### (*See* Public Inquiries)

## INSPECTION OF DOCUMENTS

### (*See also* Books and Documents—Freedom of Information)

In general terms, any requirement that a parish council

---

[1] L.G.(M.P.)A. 1976, s. 16, as amended.
[2] L.G.A. 1972, s. 142.

shall keep a document of any description is satisfied if it keeps a photographic copy of the document.[1]

The minutes of proceedings of the parish council must be open to the inspection, at all reasonable hours, of any local government elector for the parish, and he may make a copy of, or an extract from, such minutes.[2] No payment may be required.[3] There is no obligation to supply a copy to an elector.[4] These provisions also apply to the minutes of a committee where they are submitted to the council and so become, in effect, part of the council's minutes, but not otherwise. An elector may also inspect and make a copy of, or extract from, an order for payment of money made by the parish council.[5]

The accounts of the parish council and of its treasurer shall be open to the inspection of any member of the council, at all reasonable hours, without payment, and any such member may make a copy of, or extract from, the accounts.[6]

At the audit, the accounts, together with all books and documents relating thereto, may be inspected by any persons interested. Any such person is at liberty to make copies of, or extracts from, the deposited accounts and documents without payment.[7] The auditor must also give to any local government elector for the area, who so requests, an opportunity for that elector, or his representative, to question the auditor about the accounts.[8]

---

[1] L.G.A. 1972, s. 229.
[2] L.G.A. 1972, s. 228(1).
[3] L.G.A. 1972, s. 228(6).
[4] *Russell-Walker v Gimblett*, Chichester Crown Court, 30th March 1984.
[5] L.G.A. 1972, s. 228(2).
[6] L.G.A. 1972, s. 228(3).
[7] A.C.A. 1998, s. 15(1); P.A.W.A. 2004, s. 30(1).
[8] A.C.A. 1998, s. 15(2); P.A.W.A. 2004, s. 30(2).

Any report by an auditor on the accounts must accompany the agenda for the meeting at which the parish council consider the report, and must not be excluded from material provided to the press.[1]

Any person having the custody of any of the above documents, who obstructs any person entitled to inspect or make a copy of, or extracts from, them is liable, on summary conviction, to a fine not exceeding level 1 on the standard scale for summary offences (currently £200).[2]

## INSPECTION OF PARISH PROPERTY

It is a useful practice for parish councils to arrange periodic inspections of property and equipment. An up-to-date inspection book in the form of a summarised inventory with columns for each inspection is useful. Some parish councils make such inspections the duty of the vice-chairman.

## INSURANCE

The importance of adequate insurance of parish councils against third party risks was underlined by a case in which a boy was awarded heavy damages in respect of injury sustained while playing in a playground belonging to the council.[3] Similar liability may arise in many ways in connection with a parish council's various functions, and it may be advisable to cover all such risks by a single public liability policy. Cover up to at least £5 million should be taken.

Care should be taken to see that the buildings and other

---

[1] A.C.A. 1998, s. 10; P.A.W.A. 2004, s. 22.
[2] L.G.A. 1972, s. 228(7), as amended.
[3] *Bates v. Stone Parish Council* [1954] 3 All E.R. 38.

property of the council are sufficiently insured against fire and other risks. The cover should extend to the current cost of replacing the building, for which purpose annual valuations may be necessary.

Fidelity security is required to be taken by the council in respect of the treasurer.[1] Similar security is desirable in respect of other officers. This is usually done by way of a fidelity guarantee policy.

A parish council must insure against employers' liability claims.[2] (*See* "Employees".)

Parish councils are empowered to insure against personal accidents, whether fatal or not, met with by their members while engaged on the business of the council.[3] Any sum received by the council under such insurance, after deduction of expenses of recovery, if any, is to be paid to the member concerned or his personal representatives. Insurances may also be taken out for voluntary assistants.[4]

Regular attention to insurance cover in the light of inflation is essential and, as a matter of good practice, insurance cover review should be on the agenda for the annual meeting of the council. Particular care should be taken where the insurance cover is piecemeal, since parish councils often find to their cost that some item which was thought to be covered, e.g. impact damage, is not, in fact, covered.

## INTEREST IN CONTRACT OR OTHER MATTERS

### (See Code of Conduct)

---

[1] L.G.A. 1972, s. 114.
[2] Employers' Liability (Compulsory Insurance) Act 1969.
[3] L.G.A. 1972, s. 140(1), as substituted by L.G.(M.P.)A. 1982, s. 39(1).
[4] L.G.A. 1972, s. 140A, inserted by L.G.(M.P.)A. 1982, s. 39(2).

## INVESTMENT

Any capital monies held by a parish council as the result of any sale of property, or the establishment of any fund (*see* "Funds and Accumulations") may, pending its use for statutory purposes, be invested. A parish council has a general power to invest its funds for purposes connected with its functions and for the prudent management of its affairs. The Secretary of State may issue regulations and guidance on the matter, to which the council must have regard. The former Office of the Deputy Prime Minister issued guidance in March 2004. (The O.D.P.M's functions were transferred to the D.C.L.G in May 2006.)[1]

## JOINT COMMITTEES
### (*See also* Interest in Contract or Other Matters)

A parish council may arrange with any other local authority with which it has, or may obtain, concurrent powers, for the appointment of a joint committee for the purpose of exercising a function,[2] and such a committee may have all the powers of an appointing council except the power to borrow, or to precept for a rate.[3]

Every member of a joint committee who at the time of his appointment was a member of the parish council or other appointing authority, upon ceasing to be a member of the appointing authority, ceases also to be a member of the joint committee.[4]

The expenses of the joint committee are defrayed by the

---

[1] L.G.A. 2003, ss. 12 and 15.
[2] L.G.A. 1972, s. 102.
[3] L.G.A. 1972, s. 101(6).
[4] L.G.A. 1972, s. 102(5).

councils by whom the joint committee is appointed in such proportions as they may agree upon, or as may be determined in case of difference by the district or unitary council, if the joint committee comprises only parish councils, or in any other case by a single arbitrator agreed upon by the appointing authorities, or in default of agreement, by the Secretary of State.[1]

The accounts of a joint committee are subject to audit as provided for by the Audit Commission Act 1998 and the Public Audit (Wales) Act 2004. (*See* "Audit".)

## LAND

**(See Allotments—Compulsory Purchase of Land—Information about Land—Property of Parish Council—Untidy Land)**

## LAUNDERETTES

**(See Baths, etc.)**

## LAVATORIES, PUBLIC

**(See Public Conveniences)**

## LEGAL ADVICE

Legal advice is provided free of charge by the National Association of Local Councils (109 Great Russell Street, London WC1B 3LD) and the Local Councils Advisory Service (3 Trinity Close, 20 Church Street, Henley-on-

---

[1] L.G.A. 1972, s. 103.

Thames, Oxon. RG9 1SE) for subscribing member councils. Advice may also be sought from solicitors on a fee-paying basis.

As an incident of the functions with which Parliament has entrusted them, parish councils may incur reasonable expenses on any legal matters relating to any of their powers and duties. To this end the parish council may wish to engage a local solicitor. This is particularly important where the matter has progressed beyond the advice stage, and proceedings are envisaged (*see* "Legal Proceedings"), or takes the form of a land transaction, or requires detailed local examination or prolonged local involvement.

## LEGAL PROCEEDINGS

### (*See also* Public Inquiries)

Where a parish council considers it expedient for the promotion or protection of the interest of the inhabitants of the parish, it may prosecute or defend or appear in any legal proceedings.[1]

The clerk, or any other officer or member authorised generally, or in respect of any particular matter, by resolution of the parish council, may institute or defend or appear on its behalf in proceedings before any magistrates' court.[2] Any member or officer so authorised shall be entitled to institute or defend such proceedings and to conduct the proceedings although he is not a practising solicitor.[3]

A parish council may appear and represent its inhabitants at any public or local inquiry held by any government

---

[1] L.G.A. 1972, s. 222(1)(a).
[2] L.G.A. 1972, s. 111.
[3] L.G.A. 1972, s. 223.

department or public body under any Act.[1] (*See* "Public Inquiries".)

For action in respect of damage to street furniture, *see* "Damage".

## LEGAL PROCEEDINGS IN RESPECT OF DISQUALIFICATIONS

**(See Disqualifications for Office of Parish Councillor)**

## LIBRARIES

**(See Public Libraries, Museums and Art Galleries)**

## LICENCES

Where a district or unitary council proposes to adopt powers relating to the issue of hackney carriage licences, it must first inform the parish council.[2]

If the parish council is proposing to organise a public event, e.g. a dance, theatre, etc., or any public function involving the sale of intoxicating liquor, it must take care to obtain any necessary licence.

The Licensing Act 2003 introduced a new system of licensing for the sale of alcohol and the provision of public entertainment. The topic is a large one and outside the scope of this book. The former duty to notify parish councils of certain types of licensing application has been abolished. Instead, there is general obligation to give public notice

---

[1]  L.G.A. 1972, s. 222(1)(b).
[2]  L.G.A. 1972, Sch. 14, para. 25; L.G.(M.P.)A. 1976, s. 45.

of applications, in response to which parish councils may make objections or representations.[1]

## LIFE-SAVING APPARATUS

A parish council is empowered to provide life-saving appliances at such places, whether used for bathing or not, as it thinks fit.[2]

## LIGHTING

For any highway which is the responsibility of the highway authority, the power of providing road lighting rests with the highway authority.[3] Road lighting is any lighting other than footway lighting (*see below*). On the 1st April 1967, all road lighting in a parish was transferred to the highway authority.[4] This included all lamps and other apparatus.

Usually the highway authority will be the county council and road lighting powers can be delegated by that authority to a lighting authority (i.e. a district council or parish council). The lighting authority acts as agent for the highway authority, which can control all aspects of work and expenditure.[5]

Where there is a unitary council, the highway authority will be that council, and powers of delegation will be restricted to the parish council as lighting authority.

---

[1] Licensing Act 2003 (Premises Licences and Club Premises Certificates) Regulations 2005 (S.I. No. 42). See *Alcohol and Entertainment Licensing: A Practical Guide*, Shaw & Sons Ltd., 2006.
[2] P.H.A. 1936, s. 234, and L.G.A. 1972, Sch. 14, para. 18.
[3] H.A. 1980, s. 97.
[4] H.A. 1980, s. 270.
[5] H.A. 1980, s. 98.

Footway lighting is lighting where either no lamp is more than 13 feet above the ground or no lamp is more than 20 feet above the ground and there is at least one space exceeding 50 yards between two adjacent lights in the system. This definition can be altered by Ministerial Order.[1]

A parish council is a lighting authority and may provide footway lighting.[2] The parish council may, for the purpose of lighting the roads and other public places, provide and maintain such lamps, lamp posts and other materials and apparatus as it thinks necessary, and erect or install them on or against any premises or in other convenient places. The parish council may contract with any person for the supply of gas, electricity or other means of lighting, and may employ persons for maintenance and superintendence, with or without remuneration. (For the definition of "road", *see* "Roads".) Before installing any *new* system of footway lighting, the parish council must obtain the consent of the highway authority, and this consent may be given without conditions, or subject to such conditions as the highway authority thinks fit.[3]

Where the district council, or if there is no district council, the county council, exercises lighting powers in a parish or part thereof, its expenses are charged to the whole district, or county as the case may be, unless the district (or county) council by resolution declares the expenses to be "special expenses" chargeable separately on that parish or part (*see* "Expenses").

There are two cases in which a parish council exercising footway lighting powers can compel the highway authority

---

[1]  H.A. 1980, s. 270.
[2]  P.C.A. 1957, s. 3, and L.G.A. 1972, Sch. 14, para. 34.
[3]  H.A. 1980, s. 301.

to take over its existing lighting. First, it can alter its system so that it ceases to conform to the definition of footway lighting (*see above* for definition). The second is if the highway authority proposes to provide road lighting along the same stretch as is covered by existing footway lighting and gives notice accordingly.[1]

A parish council can also light an open space under its control.[2] The conditions applicable to footway lighting do not apply.

The carrying out of the lighting powers may be exercised by a committee or officer appointed by the parish council (*see* "Agency").

The installation of lighting apparatus is subject to various consents (*see* "Consents, etc. under the Parish Councils Act 1957"); and to the same provisions relating to access to telegraphic lines, sewers, etc. as apply to bus shelters (*see* "Bus Shelters").

The parish council may fix lights or wires to a building with the consent of the owner (which includes a tenant with at least five years of his tenancy left). The owner may require the temporary removal of the equipment during reconstruction or repair of the building, and a fresh owner can require their permanent removal. If the council think a requirement of permanent removal is unreasonable, they may apply to a magistrates' court who may extend the period of notice allowed, or permit the permanent retention of the equipment either unconditionally or subject to conditions (including provision for payment of rent). Where the building is an ancient monument or an historic building, an appeal against a notice lies to the

---

[1] H.A. 1980, s. 270.
[2] O.S.A. 1906, s. 10, and P.C.A. 1957, s. 8(1).

Secretary of State and, where it is owned by certain public bodies, the appeal lies to the appropriate Minister.[1]

Where damage to any lighting apparatus is caused by negligence, the parish council may take proceedings for damages, either in the magistrates' court or the county court, depending on the sum involved. On a prosecution for criminal damage, a magistrates' court may, on conviction, order the offender to pay compensation in addition to any fine or other punishment (*see* "Damage").

A parish council may combine with any other parish council for the purpose of exercising these powers, e.g. in relation to a road forming the boundary between the parishes; may contribute towards the expenses of any other council in the exercise of such powers; and may contribute towards the reasonable expenses incurred by any person in providing public lighting.

A parish council may borrow money for public lighting purposes (*see* "Loans to Parish Council").

Basically, a stretch of road which is lighted by lamps not more than 200 yards apart is automatically subject to a speed limit, but the Road Traffic Acts contain provisions for modifying this rule in relation to particular stretches of road. In practice, these modifications frequently apply.

## LIMITS UPON THE POWERS OF THE PARISH COUNCIL

This book notes all the various powers possessed by parish councils. A parish council is a body constituted under powers conferred by Parliament and it only has the powers

---

[1] P.H.A. 1961. s. 45.

which Parliament has specifically conferred upon it by Acts of Parliament.

From time to time, a parish council is pressed to undertake an activity for which Parliament has not directly conferred the necessary powers – for example, to undertake a postcard poll of the views of residents on some public issue. If the council is satisfied that what is proposed is for the benefit of the area or its inhabitants, it may be able to use its power to incur minor expenditure (*see* "Free Resource"), but the proposal may be on too large a scale for that. An "eligible" parish council in England may be able to exercise its powers in relation to the promotion of well-being (*see* "Promotion of Well-Being"). Sometimes the proposed activity is not within the powers of *any* local authority. In such a case, the only course is to advise those who press for this undertaking accordingly, and refer them to their Member of Parliament. In other cases, Parliament has conferred the powers upon some other local authority than the parish council, usually the district council or the county council, and the powers have not been delegated to the parish council. In such a case it is important to make plain to those who demand action with which local authority the responsibility lies. If the members of the parish council are sufficiently impressed with the need for the proposed provision, it is open to the chairman to communicate with the chairman of the appropriate committee of the local authority concerned.

The sympathy and interest of the appropriate member for the area on the district council or the county council can very properly be sought.

Owing to the powers of delegation which may or may not be used in any particular area and the fact that there has been an increase in concurrent powers, i.e. powers which may be exercised by either authority, it is not easy to set out briefly the respective responsibilities of the principal councils, i.e. the county council and the district council. However, in general, the county council deals with education, highways and private streets, police, fire, personal social services, youth employment, libraries, consumer protection, refuse disposal and small holdings. The district council is responsible for housing, environmental health and nuisances, by-laws, clean air, planning applications, building regulations, coast protection, licensing, markets, refuse collection, the council tax and non-domestic rating.

Unitary councils combine all the above functions.

In most instances, the district council (or county council if there is no district council) has powers concurrently with the parish council. Unless there is a specific provision to the contrary, any of the functions of a county or district council may be delegated to a parish council (*see* "Agency").

## LITIGATION

### (See Damage—Legal Proceedings—Public Inquiries)

## LITTER

### (See *also* Untidy Land)

Legislation in respect of litter is now consolidated in the Environmental Protection Act 1990. It is a criminal offence for any person to throw down, drop or otherwise deposit any litter in, into, or from any place (whether on land or water) to which the public are entitled to or permitted to have access without payment, provided that it is in the open air or in a covered place open to the air on at least one side (such as a bus shelter).[1] If the parish council decides to prosecute, the council may resolve that any member or officer (whether or not he is a lawyer) may appear on its behalf in a magistrates' court (*see* "Legal Proceedings").

The maximum fine is fixed at level 4 on the standard scale (currently £2,500) and the court should take into account the nature of the litter and any danger which it presents to persons or animals. A parish council, with a view to promoting the abatement of litter, may take such steps as it considers appropriate to advise the public of these litter laws.

A parish council may provide litter bins in any street or public place. If it does so, it must empty and cleanse them so that the contents shall not become a nuisance or give reasonable ground for complaint. Anywhere where it may provide bins it may put up notices about the leaving of refuse and litter.

It may also cleanse and empty litter bins provided by anyone else. The county and district councils have similar powers, so where it is convenient for one authority to provide the bins and another to empty them this can be done. It should, however, be noted that the authority which provides the bins has a duty to empty them.

The county council may contribute to the expenses of the parish council in this regard. The parish council may contribute to the reasonable expenses incurred by anyone else in doing anything which the parish council could do under these provisions and two parish councils may combine for the purpose of exercising these powers, or one may contribute to the expenses of another.

---

[1] Environmental Protection Act 1990, s. 87, as amended by C.N.A.E.A. 2005.

Some firms will provide bins free in return for a right to place an advertisement on them; such advertisements need to be considered for their effect on amenity, but in many places they will not be harmful to amenity if placed inside and just below the rim at the back, where they can be seen by persons depositing litter in the bin.

A parish council has power to issue fixed penalty notices for dropping litter in accordance with conditions prescribed by the Secretary of State in relation to the authorisation of persons to give such notices.[1] These conditions have been prescribed in the Environmental Offences (Fixed Penalties) (Miscellaneous Provisions) Regulations 2007 (for England) and the Environmental Offences (Fixed Penalties) (Wales) Regulations 2008 (for Wales)[2] and require an authorised person to have successfully completed an approved course of training by an approved training provider. D.E.F.R.A. has issued guidance to parish councils in *Getting to grips with the Clean Neighbourhoods and Environment Act 2005 – a parish council guide* which can be viewed on the D.E.F.R.A. website. D.E.F.R.A. has also arranged for training to be provided for those local council officers who will enforce the provisions of the Act. Details of the training courses can be found on the Keep Britain Tidy website www.keepbritaintidy.org/Expertise/Training/Default.aspx.

The dumping on any land in the open air (even on another's private land) or on a highway, of a motor vehicle or any part thereof, or on any such land anything other than a motor vehicle, is an offence for which the maximum penalty is a fine at level 4 on the standard scale for summary offences (currently £2,500) or 3 months' imprisonment or both. The offence may also be punished by a fixed penalty (currently

---

[1] Environmental Protection Act 1990, s. 88, as amended by C.N.A.E.A, s. 19.
[2] S.I. 175 and S.I. 663 respectively.

£200). A parish council may prosecute.[1] The district or unitary council must provide places for the free dumping of rubbish.[2] The district or unitary council must deal with abandoned motor vehicles and may remove other dumped refuse.[3]

## LOANS TO PARISH COUNCIL

In general, a parish council may borrow money for any purpose or class of purpose approved by the Secretary of State, and in accordance with any conditions subject to which the approval is given.[4]

In practice, applications for loans in England should be made to the National Association of Local Councils through the County Association, since the Secretary of State has delegated administration of loan applications to the Association.

There was formerly a ceiling on the total amount councils could borrow in any one financial year. That ceiling has been abolished but an individual council will not normally be authorised to borrow more than £500,000 in a single year.

In Wales, the system is slightly different. A council may apply either through its Association (*see* "One Voice Wales") or direct to the Local Government Finance Division of the National Assembly for Wales. There is no specific limit to the amount a council may borrow but the National Assembly may set an annual cash limit on the total available for borrowing.

---

[1] Refuse Disposal (Amenity) Act 1978, ss. 2 and 2A (the latter inserted by C.N.A.E.A, s. 10).
[2] *ibid.*, s. 1.
[3] *ibid.*, ss. 3 to 6.
[4] L.G.A. 2003, Sch. 1, para. 2.

Money can be raised in various ways – by mortgage, the issue of stock, etc., by an agreement with the U.K. Debt Management Office and by any other means approved by the Secretary of State. Mostly, councils borrow from the Public Works Loans Board which operates (as does the Debt Management Office) from Eastcheap Court, 11 Philpot Lane, London EC3M 8UD (website www.dmo.gov.uk).

Reborrowing for the purpose of paying monies borrowed, or borrowing by way of temporary loan or overdraft from a bank or otherwise pending the receipt of revenue or authorised loan capital, does not require the approval of the Secretary of State.

All money borrowed by a parish council must be charged indifferently on all the revenues of the authority, and all securities created rank equally without any priority.

Two or more local authorities may combine to exercise their powers of borrowing.

The Secretary of State has made regulations on matters of detail relating to borrowing – see the Local Authorities (Capital Finance and Accounting) (England) Regulations 2003[1] and the Local Authorities (Capital Finance and Accounting) (Wales) Regulations 2003.[2]

## LOCAL ACT POWERS

The powers and duties of parish councils set out in this book are those contained in the general law. It should not be forgotten, however, that some parish councils have,

---

[1] S.I. 3146, as amended.

[2] S.I. 3239, as amended

in addition, power conferred on them by Private Acts. Parish councils have no power themselves to promote Bills in Parliament (*see* "Bills in Parliament"), but local Bills promoted by other local authorities may contain provisions conferring powers on parish councils. In recent years a number of parish councils have obtained powers not available under the general law, under county council Acts. The 1972 Act provided for the then existing Local Acts to be phased out but Local Acts passed after 1st April 1974 remain in force. (*See* "Bills in Parliament".)

## LOCAL GOVERNMENT ELECTORS

The local government electors for an area are those whose names are registered in the current register of local government electors.[1] These registers are generally combined with the registers of parliamentary electors, the names of those registered only as local government electors being specially marked.

The register is published annually no later than 1st December but subsequent changes are made as they occur, thus creating a "rolling" register that is always up to date. A person is entitled to be included in the next register if he is resident in any local government area and he is a British subject,[2] citizen of the Republic of Ireland or a citizen of a member state of the European Union of full age (18) or who will attain full age before the end of 12 months beginning with the 1st December next and is not subject to any legal incapacity to vote. His right to vote, however, depends on his achieving full age by the election day. If a local government area is divided into wards, he can only vote for the ward in which he resides. If the place at

---

[1] L.G.A. 1972, s. 270.
[2] Which includes Commonwealth citizens.

which he resides is covered by two or three different local government authorities, e.g. a county council, a district council and a parish council, he is, of course, entitled to vote at elections for all these bodies.

Those who are registered as service voters can vote by proxy. Absent voters may vote by post or by proxy.[1]

Only local government electors are entitled to speak and vote at a parish meeting. Non-electors may be invited or permitted to speak, but not to vote.

## LOCAL OMBUDSMAN

### (See Commission for Local Administration)

## LOTTERIES

A parish council may run a lottery[2] provided it has a lottery operating licence issued by the Gambling Commission. The Commission provides guidance, pamphlets and forms. Its address is Victoria Square House, Victoria Square, Birmingham B2 4BP (www.gamblingcommission.gov.uk).

## MARKETS

A parish council has a power to establish a market in its area and to acquire by agreement any existing market within its area. In pursuance of this power, the council may provide a market place and a market house or other buildings convenient for holding a market. A council cannot, however, establish a market so as to interfere with

---

[1] R.P.A. 1985, s. 8.
[2] Gaming Act 2005, s. 98.

the market rights, powers or privileges of another person without that person's consent.[1]

# MAYOR

## (See Chairman of Parish Council)

# MEETINGS OF PARISH COUNCIL

## (See *also* Annual Meeting of Parish Council—Chairman of Parish Council—Interest in Contract or Other Matters—Parish Council—Quorum)

### Frequency

A parish council in England must hold not less than four meetings in each year, of which one is to be the annual meeting.[2] A community council in Wales must hold the annual meeting and may hold such additional meetings as it thinks fit.[3]

### Open to the public

Every meeting is to be open to the public except where the council formally resolves to exclude the public (which includes the Press) from all or part of a meeting on the grounds that publicity would be prejudicial to the public interest by reason of the confidential nature of the business to be transacted or for other special reasons stated in the resolution and arising from the nature of the business or of the proceedings.[4] This provision applies equally to any committee of the parish council[5] and to the parish

---

[1] Food Act 1984, ss. 50 and 61.
[2] L.G.A. 1972, Sch. 12, para. 8.
[3] *ibid.*, para. 24.
[4] Public Bodies (Admission to Meetings) Act 1960, s. 1.
[5] L.G.A. 1972, s. 100.

meeting. The resolution (which could be challenged in the courts) must be carefully worded and reported verbatim in the minutes.

The public cannot be excluded simply on the chairman's ruling. The decision must be taken by the council. It is unwise to exclude the public or Press unless it is considered absolutely necessary since this can give rise to bad feeling and allegations of secrecy. Exclusion should be strictly limited to the period during which the specific issue which requires confidential discussion is being considered.

Where a meeting is to be open to the public, the Press must, if they ask, be given in advance a copy of the agenda and any supporting documents. From a public relations point of view it is good practice to do this even if they do not ask.

Members of the public have no rights to speak at a parish council meeting unless the council (not the chairman) authorises this. A district councillor has no special rights above those of an ordinary member of the public.

The Local Government (Access to Information) Act 1985 (contained in Part VA of the Local Government Act 1972) does not apply to parish councils as a matter of law, but they may voluntarily operate all or some of its provisions if they so wish.

### Convening

The chairman may call a meeting of the parish council at any time. Any two members may present a requisition to the chairman to convene a meeting. If the chairman thereafter refuses to call a meeting, any two members may forthwith convene one. If, without refusing, the chairman does not within seven days after the requisition convene a meeting, any two members may forthwith convene a meeting.[1]

## Notices

Three clear days[2] at least before a meeting of the parish council, a notice specifying the time and place of meeting must be posted at the offices of the council or, if it has no offices, in some conspicuous place in the parish,[3] and a summons sent to each member. If the meeting is called by members of the council, the notice must specify the business to be transacted, and must be signed by those members. A summons to attend the meeting, specifying the business to be transacted, signed by the clerk, must be left at or sent by post to the usual place of residence of every member of the council at least three clear days before the meeting. The period of three clear days is exclusive of the day on which the notice is given and the day on which the meeting is held.[4] (*See* "Notices, etc.".) Lack of service of the summons on any member does not affect the validity of a meeting.

In view of the above provisions (which are statutory), it is undesirable to discuss any business of substantial importance of which notice has not been given. In particular, no *decision* can lawfully be taken on any matter not specified in the summons, e.g. which arises under "any other business". It is useful for standing orders to specify this point to avoid difficulties.

## Place

A parish council meeting must not be held in premises which at the time of the meeting may be used for the sale

---

[1]  L.G.A. 1972, Sch. 12, paras. 9 and 25.
[2]  Saturdays and Sundays are *not* excluded.
[3]  Public Bodies (Admissions to Meetings) Act 1960, s. 1(4).
[4]  L.G.A. 1972, Sch. 12, paras. 10 and 26.

of alcohol by virtue of a premises licence or a temporary event notice under the Licensing Act 2003, except when no other suitable room is available free of charge or at a reasonable charge. There is nothing to prevent the meetings being held outside the boundaries of the parish if the council consider this course desirable.[1]

When there is no suitable public room which can be used free of charge, the parish council is entitled to use, free of charge, at all reasonable times and after reasonable notice for the purpose of a meeting of the parish council, any suitable room in a community, foundation or voluntary school, or any suitable room the expense of maintaining which is payable out of any rate. (*See* "Rooms in School and Rooms Maintained out of Rates".)

A parish council is empowered to provide or acquire buildings for public offices and for public meetings. (*See* "Public or Parish Offices".)

There is no legal reason why a meeting should not take place in a private house but the practice is undesirable since the council is conducting public business.

## Quorum

No business is to be transacted at any meeting of a parish council unless at least one-third of the full number of members are present. In no case, however, can the quorum be less than three. (*See further* "Quorum".)

## Minutes

Minutes of the proceedings of every parish council or of any committee thereof are to be kept in a book.[2] The minutes

---

[1] L.G.A. 1972, Sch. 12, paras. 10 and 26.
[2] *ibid.*, para. 41.

should be kept by the clerk. If there is no clerk, some person should be authorised by the council or committee for the purpose. Minutes should be short. In general terms they should record decisions, not the discussions which precede them. The council minutes must be signed at the same or the next ensuing meeting of the council by the presiding chairman. A loose-leaf book may be used provided that the pages are consecutively numbered and each page is initialled by the chairman when the minutes are signed. This facilitates the typing of minutes. Questions sometimes arise as to the printing of the council's minutes and reports. The circulated papers in the larger local authorities are voluminous and printing is largely used for this purpose. There is nothing to prevent a parish council taking the same course where the circumstances warrant it. For inspection of minutes, *see* "Inspection of Documents".

## Procedure

The names of members present at any council meeting must be recorded.[1] Any member may move a resolution of a matter on the agenda, which should then be discussed and voted upon. The extent and length of discussion is a matter for the chairman who should exercise a careful but firm balance between ensuring full and relevant discussions, and avoiding verbosity, irrelevant matter and repetitiveness. A seconder to a resolution is not essential, unless standing orders so provide. Except in very straightforward cases, the resolution should be noted in writing by the clerk before voting takes place to avoid the possibility of subsequent misunderstandings as to the wording. The mode of voting *must* be by show of hands unless otherwise provided in standing orders.[2] The names of members voting on each question must also be recorded

---

[1] L.G.A. 1972, Sch. 12, para. 40.

[2] *ibid.*, paras. 13 and 29.

on the requisition of any member of the council, so as to show whether each vote given was for or against the question. Hence a vote cannot be taken by secret ballot, unless standing orders so provide.

Every question must be decided by a majority of the members present and voting on the question.[1] In the case of an equal division of votes, the chairman has a second or casting vote. The chairman has an original as well as a casting vote. The manner in which each member voted must be recorded in the minutes if any member so requires either before or after the vote is taken.

A parish council may make, vary and revoke standing orders for the regulation of its proceedings and business, and of the proceedings and business at parish meetings. (*See* "Standing Orders".)

As regards disorderly conduct at meetings of parish councils, every deliberative body is empowered at common law to protect itself in its deliberations, and if these deliberations are materially obstructed by the disorderly conduct of any person thereat, whether a stranger or a member, the general body, acting through the chairman, is justified in removing that obstruction by requiring such person to leave the meeting, and if such requisition be not obeyed, by using such an amount of force as may be necessary to compel his retirement. It is desirable that any force which it may be necessary to use in any case of this kind should be applied, where the opportunity offers, by a police constable. The parish council must determine for itself how far in any particular instance there may or may not be such conduct as materially obstructs the deliberations of the council.

---

[1] L.G.A. 1972, Sch. 12, para. 39.

## MEETINGS, PARISH OR COMMUNITY

**(See Parish Meetings)**

## MEMBERS' INTERESTS

**(See Code of Conduct)**

## MEMORIALS

**(See War Memorials)**

## MINOR AND MISCELLANEOUS EXPENSES

**(See Free Resource)**

## MINUTES

**(See Meetings of Parish Council)**

## MONITORING OFFICER

The monitoring officer is an official of the district or unitary council whose function is, broadly speaking, to keep under review the ethical standards of councillors of that council, with powers to investigate councillors' conduct in specific cases. The monitoring officer is responsible for holding the register of councillors' interests (including those of parish councillors) which is required to be compiled under Part 3 of the Codes of Conduct (Appendices 1 and 2).[1]

---

[1] L.G.A. 2000, Part III, and Local Authorities (Code of Conduct) (Local Determination) Regulations 2003 (S.I. 1483), as amended.

## MONUMENTS

**(See Burial and Cremation)**

## MORTGAGES

**(See Loans to Parish Council)**

## MORTUARIES AND POST-MORTEM ROOMS

A parish council may, and if required by the Secretary of State must, provide (a) a mortuary for the reception of dead bodies before interment, and (b) a post-mortem room for the reception of dead bodies during the time required to conduct any post-mortem examination ordered by a coroner; and it may make by-laws with respect to the management, and charge for the use of any such place.[1] (*See* "By-laws".)

The council may provide for the interment of any dead body received into its mortuary, but the burial expenses are chargeable to the deceased's estate.

As to obtaining a loan, *see* "Loans to Parish Council".

Except in large parishes, mortuaries are usually provided by the district or unitary council which has the like powers and duties. Where it appears to the district or unitary council that no suitable arrangements have been made for the disposal of the body of a person who has died or been found dead in its area, it is the duty of that district council to arrange for the body to be buried or cremated.[2]

---

[1] P.H.A. 1936, s. 198.
[2] Public Health (Control of Disease) Act 1984, s. 46.

## MOTOR-CYCLE PARKS

### (*See* Parking Places)


## MUSEUMS AND ART GALLERIES

A parish council may contribute to a local museum or art gallery through its powers to contribute to the arts (*see* "Entertainment and the Arts").


## NAME AND STYLE OF PARISH

### (*See also* Signs and Signposts)

The district or unitary council may change the name of a parish at the request of the parish council, or of the parish meeting where there is no parish council. The change of name must be published in such manner as the district or unitary council directs and must be notified to the Secretary of State, the Director General of the Ordnance Survey and the Registrar General.[1]

A change of name will not affect any rights or obligations of the parish, or any pending legal proceedings.

In England, a parish council and a parish meeting where there is no council may resolve to adopt the alternative style of "community", "neighbourhood" or "village". Having done so, it may by resolution revert to being called a "parish". Where a change is made, the Secretary of State, the Office for National Statistics, the Electoral Commission and the principal council(s) in whose area the parish is situated must be informed.[2]

---

[1] L.G.A. 1972, ss. 75 (England), 76 (Wales).
[2] L.G.A. 1972, ss. 12A, 12B and 17B (inserted by L.G.P. I.H.A. 2007).

# NAMING OF STREETS

**(See Numbering of Houses and Naming of Streets)**


# NATIONAL ASSOCIATION OF LOCAL COUNCILS

The main representative body for parish councils in England is the National Association of Local Councils, 109 Great Russell Street, London WC1B 3LD, founded in 1947 (www.nalc.gov.uk). It has county associations in every county (or group of counties). For Wales, *see* "One Voice Wales".


# NATIONAL INSURANCE

**(See Employees)**


# NATIONAL PARK AUTHORITIES

In England, the Secretary of State is required to appoint a certain number of National Park Authority members from among parish councillors, and chairmen of parish meetings without councils, whose parishes are wholly or partly within National Park boundaries. The maximum number is one less than half the total number of Authority members appointed by the Secretary of State. As a general rule, just under half the Authority members are appointed by the Secretary of State, with the majority being appointed by the principal local authorities within the area of the National Park.[1]

The National Assembly is not required to appoint

---

[1] Environment Act 1995, s. 63 and Sch. 7.

community councillors as members of National Park Authorities in Wales.

# NOISE

### *(See also* Nuisances and Pollution)

District and unitary councils have wide general powers to act against noise or vibration which is a nuisance. These powers can by agreement be exercised by a parish council (*see* "Agency"). It is an offence to use loudspeakers in streets at night (i.e. between 9 p.m. and 8 a.m.) for any purpose, or at any time for commercial advertising or advertising entertainments. There are a number of exclusions from these prohibitions, ranging from police loudspeakers, loudspeakers hailing a ship and pleasure fair loudspeakers, to ordinary car radios. For offences concerning loudspeakers, the parish council has power to prosecute.[1]

The district or unitary council has power to control the use of loudspeakers in streets by adopting Schedule 2 to the Noise and Statutory Nuisance Act 1993, under which it operates a licensing system.

Under the Noise Act 1996, a district or unitary council has power to deal with complaints about excessive noise from dwellings and licensed premises at night (between 11 p.m. and 7 a.m.).

Advice may be sought from the Noise Abatement Society, Suite 2, 26 Brunswick Terrace, Hove BN3 1HJ (www. noiseabatementsociety.com).

---

[1] Control of Pollution Act 1974, s. 62.

# NOTICES BY OR TO PARISH COUNCIL OR OF PARISH MEETING

## (*See also* Meetings of Parish Council—Parish Meeting)

Any public notice required to be given by a parish council must be given by posting the notice in some conspicuous place or places in the parish and in such other manner as appears to the parish council to be desirable for giving publicity to the notice, e.g. leaflets, advertisements in local paper, etc.[1]

A public notice of a parish meeting (which may be in writing or in print, or partly in writing and partly in print) must be given as above and must specify the time and place of the meeting and the business to be transacted at the meeting, and it must be posted up seven clear days before the meeting – that is, exclusive of the day of giving the notice and the day on which the meeting is to be held. If, in England, the business relates to the establishment or dissolution of a parish council, or the grouping of a local area with another local area, not less than 14 days' notice must be given. In Wales, there are special rules relating to the calling of meetings to consider the establishment and dissolution of community councils and the grouping of communities (*see* "Parish Council – Creation of community council in Wales *and* Dissolution of community council in Wales"). The duty of giving public notice of the meeting is imposed on the chairman of the parish council, or on the conveners of the meeting, as the case may be.[2]

Public notice is required to be given by a parish council as to the audit of their accounts. (*See* "Audit".)

At least three clear days before a meeting of the parish

---

[1] L.G.A. 1972, s. 232.
[2] L.G.A. 1972, Sch. 12, paras. 15 and 30.

council, a notice must be given as above and a summons, specifying the business proposed to be transacted and signed by the clerk, left at or sent by post to the residence of every parish councillor.[1] (*See also* "Meetings of Parish Council".)

Any notice required to be given to or served on a parish council, or to or upon the clerk or chairman, shall be addressed to the council and left at or sent by prepaid post to the offices of the council.[2] In the case of notices required to be given to or served on a parish meeting, or the chairman of a parish meeting, these should be addressed to the chairman of the parish meeting at his private address.

Notice is required to be given to a parish council by a district or unitary council of the particulars of any planning application in the area of the parish council, provided the local council has requested to be notified of all such applications. (*See* "Planning".)

Parish councils and the chairmen of parish meetings in England without councils are entitled to be notified of public path creation, diversion and extinguishment orders and of orders modifying the definitive map (*see* "Highways").

Notice is required to be given by the district or unitary council to a parish council and to the chairman of a parish meeting in England without a council of the exercise of regulatory powers relating to Hackney Carriage licences (*see* "Licences"), by-laws for promenades and the seashore and street naming.[3]

Notice is to be given to the chairman of the council of any resignation by a parish councillor (*see* "Parish Councillor"),

---

[1]  L.G.A. 1972, Sch. 12, paras. 10 and 26.
[2]  L.G.A. 1972, s. 231.
[3]  L.G.A. 1972, Sch. 14, para. 25.

and a notice is to be given to the council by the chairman in the event of his resigning his chairmanship (*see* "Chairman of Parish Council").[1]

## NUISANCES AND POLLUTION

**(*See also* Ditches and Drains—Noise)**

Nuisances and cases of pollution should be reported to the district or unitary council for attention and action. If, however, the district or unitary council refuses to take appropriate action, the parish council has two reserve powers available to it under the Environmental Protection Act 1990, Part III. First, it may advise private persons particularly affected to take proceedings in a magistrates' court for an abatement order and, if the nuisance affects the parish in general, contribute to the costs of the private persons' court case out of the free resource. Second, it can report the failure to the Environment Agency, which has powers to investigate.

## NUMBERING OF HOUSES AND NAMING OF STREETS

A parish council has no direct powers in this field, since it is a duty imposed on the district or unitary council.[2] The district or unitary council can arrange for the parish council to carry out this function, but only if the parish council agrees.[3] If this happens, the parish council acts as agent and the district or unitary council must pay the cost. The district or unitary council could, however, declare the expenses to be special expenses chargeable to the parish.

[1] L.G.A. 1972, s. 84.
[2] Town Improvement Clauses Act 1847, s. 64; P.H.A. 1925, ss. 17-19.
[3] L.G.A. 1972, s. 101.

# OBSTRUCTION OF HIGHWAY

**(See Highways)**

# OFFICERS OF PARISH COUNCIL

**(See Clerk of Parish Council—Deputy Officers— Employees—Gratuities to Officers—Legal Proceedings— Superannuation of Paid Officers—Treasurer of Parish Council)**

# OFFICES FOR PARISH COUNCIL

**(See Land—Property of Parish Council—Public or Parish Offices)**

# OMBUDSMAN

**(See Commission for Local Administration)**

# ONE VOICE WALES

The national representative body for community councils in Wales is One Voice Wales (Un Llais Cymru), 24 College Street, Ammanford SA18 3AF (www.onevoicewales.org.uk).

# OPEN SPACES

The powers which may be exercised by a parish with respect to an "open space" which is under its control, or to the expense of which it has contributed, to however small an extent, are similar to those in respect of a recreation ground.[1] (*See* "Recreation".)

---

[1] P.H.A. 1875, s. 164, and L.G.A. 1972, Sch. 14, para. 27.

Under the Open Spaces Act 1906, trustees under a local Act may transfer any open space to a parish council so that the open space may be preserved for the enjoyment of the public, or may enter into an agreement with the parish council for the opening to the public of the open space and for the care and management of the same by the parish council.[1] Where an open space is vested in trustees for any charitable purpose, and the open space is no longer required for the purpose of the trust, the trustees may transfer the open space to the parish council.[2]

A parish council may acquire and undertake the management of any open space or disused burial ground.[3] It must maintain it in a good and decent state. Any land held by a parish council under the 1906 Act is held on a statutory trust for the public. This is not necessarily a charitable trust.[4]

A parish council may make by-laws for the regulation of any open space. (*See* "By-laws".)

An "open space" is defined in the Act of 1906 as "any land, whether enclosed or not, on which there are no buildings or of which not more than one-twentieth part is covered with buildings, and the whole or the remainder of which is laid out as a garden or is used for purposes of recreation, or lies waste and unoccupied".[5] Several of the provisions of the Act also apply to disused burial grounds.

A parish council may borrow money for the purposes of the Act of 1906. (*See* "Loans to Parish Council".)

The address of the Open Spaces Society, which may be

---

[1] O.S.A. 1906, s. 2.
[2] O.S.A. 1906, s. 4.
[3] O.S.A. 1906, s. 9.
[4] O.S.A. 1906, s. 10.
[5] O.S.A. 1906, s. 20.

able to advise a council with a problem, is 25A Bell Street, Henley-on-Thames, Oxon. RG9 2BA (www.oss.org.uk).

# PARISH

Subject to adjustments in a few cases, all rural parishes in England in existence immediately before 1st April 1974 continued to exist as parishes,[1] together with those former urban districts or boroughs, or parts thereof, constituted as parishes by order of the Secretary of State with effect from 1st April 1974.[2]

In Wales, all rural parishes in existence immediately before 1st April 1974 ceased to exist as local areas, but were reborn on that date under the name of communities (*see* "Community").

Since 1974 further changes have been made in respect of both parishes and communities as a result of reviews undertaken by principal councils, the Local Government Commission and its successor, the Electoral Commission (*see* "Alteration of Areas").

# PARISH COUNCIL

**(See *also* Annual Meeting of Parish Council—Expenses—Grouping of Parishes—Legal Proceedings—Meetings of Parish Council—Parish Councillor—Quorum—Town Council)**

## Definition

There are over 9,000 parish and community councils in England and Wales.

---

[1] L.G.A. 1972, s. 1(6).
[2] L.G.A. 1972, Sch. 1, Part V.

These include, in England, parish councils whether separate or common which were already in existence on 1st April 1974,[1] former rural borough councils which became parish councils on that date, and former borough and urban district councils given "successor" status as parish councils by the Secretary of State.[2]

In Wales, these include former parish councils which became community councils on 1st April 1974 and former borough and urban district councils which became community councils by order of the Secretary of State.[3] The term "parish council", as used herein, includes community councils unless otherwise stated.

A parish council is a corporate body, but it is not necessary for it to have a common seal. Any parish council act which requires a seal, e.g. a deed of conveyance, should be signed and sealed by two members of the council.[4] A parish council is a local authority.[5] For a parish council becoming a town council, *see* "Town Council".

## Creation of parish council in England

In any parish in England where no parish council exists, the district, unitary or London borough council may establish a parish council as part of a community governance review (*see* "Alteration of Areas"). If the parish has 1,000 or more local government electors, the review must recommend that the parish should have a council. If the number of electors is less than 1,000 and more than 150, the review may so recommend. If the number of electors is 150 or

---

[1] L.G.A. 1972, s. 9.
[2] L.G.A. 1972, Sch. 1, Part V.
[3] L.G.A. 1972, s. 27.
[4] L.G.A. 1972, ss. 14 and 33.
[5] L.G.A. 1972, s. 270.

fewer, the review must recommend that the parish should not have a council.[1]

For the creation of parishes and parish councils by petition, *see* "Alteration of Areas".

## Creation of community council in Wales

A community meeting which does not have a separate council may apply to the county or county borough council for the establishment of a community council for the community. However, an application may only be made if (a) a poll of local government electors for the community has been held and (b) a majority of those voting in the poll supports the application. The decision to hold a poll must be made at a community meeting at which at least 30% of the electorate or, if that number exceeds 300, at least 300 electors, are present. At least 30 clear days' notice of the meeting must be given.[2]

If the above conditions are met, the county or county borough council is obliged to establish the council by order and make provision for the election of councillors, etc.

## Dissolution of parish council in England

Where in England the population of a parish having a separate parish council includes not more than 150 local government electors, the parish meeting may apply to the district or London borough council for that council to make an order dissolving the parish council. If such an application is rejected, a further application cannot be made for two years.[3]

---

[1] L.G.P. I.H.A. 2007, s. 94.
[2] L.G.A. 1972, ss. 28-29B, Sch. 12, para. 30(2).
[3] L.G.A. 1972, s. 10.

## Dissolution of community council in Wales

The procedure for dissolving a community council is essentially the same as for its creation and, if successfully followed, obliges the county or county borough council to dissolve the community council and make provision for the winding up of its affairs.

If a proposal to create or dissolve a community council is rejected in a poll, a further poll cannot be held for at least two years. Furthermore, such a proposal cannot be made for two years (a) after changes made to the communities in question following a review by the Local Government Boundary Commission for Wales, or (b) following a successful application for a creation or a dissolution order.[1]

## Size of council

A parish council in England consists of such number of councillors as may be fixed from time to time by the district or unitary council, not being less than five.[2] There is no similar provision for fixing the size of a community council in Wales but in practice it is not less than five.

If a casual vacancy arises, the parish council must fill the vacancy by co-option, except that there must be a by-election if a poll is claimed (*see* "Election and Appointment of Parish Councillors").

The proceedings of a council are not to be invalidated by any vacancy among the members, or by any defect in the election or qualification of any of the members.[3]

For changes to the size of a council through a community governance review, *see* "Alteration of Areas".

---

[1] L.G.A. 1972, ss. 28-30.
[2] L.G.A. 1972, s. 16(1).
[3] L.G.A. 1972, s. 82.

# PARISH COUNCILLOR

**(See also Allowances to Parish Councillors—
Disqualifications for Office of Parish Councillor—
Election and Appointment of Parish Councillors—
Interest in Contract or Other Matters—Meetings of
Parish Council)**

A parish councillor must be aged 18 years[1] or over, be a British subject,[2] a citizen of the Irish Republic or a citizen of a member state of the European Union and be (1) a local government elector of the parish; or (2) a person who (a) has, during the whole of the 12 months before he was nominated as a candidate, occupied land or other premises as owner or tenant in the parish, or (b) has, during the same period, resided in that area or within three miles thereof, or (c) has, during the same period, had his principal or only place of work in that area.[3]

It has been decided that, in order to constitute residence, a person must possess at least a sleeping apartment, but that an uninterrupted abiding at such dwelling is not essential. A person may be resident in more than one place at the same time, e.g. a college student.[4] "Work" includes the performance of the duties of a councillor, so that a councillor seeking re-election qualifies as a candidate by virtue of acting as a councillor.[5]

Where a member of the council ceases to be qualified to be a member, the council must forthwith declare his office vacant and signify the vacancy by notice signed by the clerk and publicly notified (*see* "Notices").

---

[1] The age was reduced from 21 by the Electoral Administration Act 2006, s. 17.
[2] Which includes a Commonwealth citizen.
[3] L.G.A. 1972, s. 79.
[4] *Fox v. Stirk* [1970] 2 Q.B. 463.
[5] *Parker v. Yeo* [1992] 90 L.G.R. 645.

As to who are local government electors, *see* "Local Government Electors".

In the case of parish councils in England, the number of councillors is as may be fixed from time to time by the district council but must not be less than five.

For the election and term of office of a parish councillor and the position if casual vacancies arise, *see* "Election and Appointment of Parish Councillors".

A councillor, by notice in writing to the chairman (N.B. not to the clerk), may resign his office. Resignation takes effect on receipt of the notice by the chairman.[1]

Every parish councillor, before or at the next meeting after his election or, if the council at the first meeting so permits, then at a later meeting fixed by the council, must make in the presence of some member of the council or a proper officer of the council (i.e. usually the clerk) and deliver to the council a declaration of acceptance of office in the form prescribed which includes an undertaking to observe the council's code of conduct in the performance of his duties (*see* "Code of Conduct").[2] If he fails to do so his office is void and a casual vacancy automatically arises.[3]

A parish councillor may be appointed as clerk or treasurer of the council *without remuneration*. A person who is or has been a member of the parish council is disqualified from being appointed by the council to any paid office whilst he is a member and for a period of 12 months after he has ceased to be a member.[4]

Parish councillors are not exempt from jury service.

---

[1] L.G.A. 1972, s. 84.
[2] L.G.A. 1972, s. 83 and L.G.A. 2000, s. 52.
[3] L.G.A. 1972, s. 83.
[4] L.G.A. 1972, s. 102.

As to the payments which may be made to parish councillors in respect of their personal expenses and financial losses as a result of council work, *see* "Allowances to Parish Councillors".

A person, if duly qualified, may be elected as a parish councillor for more than one parish or community.

A parish councillor has no personal financial liability in respect of anything done *in good faith* for the purpose of any of the council's statutory functions.[1]

## PARISH MEETING

### (*See also* Chairman of Parish Meeting—Community— Quorum—Wards)

Unless otherwise stated, what is set out below in respect of parish meetings applies to community meetings in Wales and town meetings in both England and Wales.

The persons entitled to speak and vote at a parish meeting are the persons registered as local government electors for the parish.[2]

The chairman of a parish council is entitled to attend a parish meeting for the parish (or where a grouping order is in force, for any of the parishes comprised in the group) whether or not he is a local government elector for the parish.[3] If the parish has a separate parish council, the chairman of that council, if present, shall preside at a parish meeting and, in the case of English meetings only, if he is absent the vice-chairman (if any) shall preside; but, if he is

---

[1] L.G.(M.P.)A. 1976, s. 39.
[2] L.G.A. 1972, ss. 13(1) and 32(1).
[3] L.G.A. 1972, Sch. 12, paras. 16 and 31.

not a local government elector for the parish or community, he is not entitled to give any vote except a casting vote as chairman. In the absence of the chairman (in Wales) or the chairman and vice-chairman (in England) of the parish council, a parish meeting may appoint another person to take the chair for the occasion and that person has all the powers and authority of a chairman. (*See* "Chairman of Parish Meeting".)

There is no obligation on the chairman or other members of a parish council to attend a parish meeting, although it is usual for them to do so.

In a parish in England not having a separate parish council, the parish meeting chooses a chairman for the year at its annual assembly (*see below*). If that chairman is absent from any meeting during that year, the meeting may appoint another person to take the chair and that person has all the powers and authority of a chairman. In a community in Wales not having a separate community council, the meeting must appoint a person for the occasion only. (*See* "Chairman of Parish Meeting".)

Members of the public (including the Press) may be present at the parish meeting, notwithstanding that they are not local government electors for the parish but they have no right to take part in the business of the meeting.[1] They may only be excluded by a formal resolution of the parish meeting (for the circumstances in which the public can be excluded, *see* "Meetings of Parish Council").

The parish meeting in England must assemble annually on some day between 1st March and 1st June, both dates inclusive. In the case of a parish not having a separate parish council, the parish meeting must assemble at least

---

[1] Public Bodies (Admission to Meetings) Act 1960, s. 1.

twice a year. Subject to these rules, parish meetings in England may be held on such days and at such times and places as may be fixed by the parish council or, if there is no parish council, by the chairman of the parish meeting.[1] The community meeting in Wales is *not* required to assemble annually or at all. Proceedings at a parish meeting must not begin earlier than six o'clock in the evening.[2]

A parish meeting in England, but not a community meeting in Wales, may arrange for the discharge of any of its functions by a committee of local government electors for the parish but any such arrangement does not prevent the parish meeting itself from exercising these functions. The acts of a committee do not need ratification by the parish meeting.[3]

In England, the chairman of the parish council, or any two parish councillors or, if there is no parish council, the chairman of the parish meeting or any person representing the parish on the district council may convene a parish meeting, or any six local government electors may at any time convene a parish meeting.[4]

In Wales, the chairman of the community council or any two councillors of that council, or any six local government electors may at any time convene a community meeting.[5]

Seven clear days' (i.e. nine days') notice of the holding of a parish meeting must be given. If, in England, the business transacted relates to the establishment or dissolution of a parish council, or to the grouping of the parish with another parish under a common parish council, at least 14

---

[1] L.G.A. 1972, Sch. 12, para. 15.
[2] *ibid.*, paras. 14 and 32.
[3] L.G.A. 1972, s. 108.
[4] L.G.A. 1972, Sch. 12, para. 15.
[5] *ibid.*, para. 30.

days' notice of the meeting must be given. In Wales, the law is different (*see* "Grouping of Parishes – Wales" and "Parish Councils – Creation and dissolution of community councils in Wales". The duty of giving public notice of the meeting is imposed on the chairman of the parish council, or on the conveners of the meeting, as the case may be. The person(s) convening the meeting must sign the notice. (*See* "Notices, etc.")

A parish meeting must not be held in premises which at the time of the meeting may be used for the sale of alcohol by virtue of a premises licence or a temporary event notice under the Licensing Act 2003, except where no other suitable room is available either free of charge or at a reasonable cost.[1] As to the use of schoolrooms, etc., *see* "Rooms in School and Rooms Maintained out of Rates".

Minutes of the proceedings of every parish meeting must be kept in a book provided for that purpose, and shall be signed at the same or the next ensuing assembly of the parish meeting or meeting of the committee, as the case may be, by the person presiding thereat. Until the contrary is proved, a parish meeting in respect of the proceedings of which a minute has been so made and signed is deemed to have been duly convened and held and all the persons present at the meeting are deemed to have been duly qualified.[2] Differences of opinion sometimes arise as to whether it is part of the duty of the clerk to the parish council to take the minutes of a parish meeting. There is no simple answer to this, although a good working rule is that he is obliged to do so if it has been the practice for his predecessors to do so. The simplest solution is for the clerk to have a short written contract, specifying his duties

[1] L.G.A. 1972, Sch. 12, paras. 14 and 32.
[2] *ibid.*, paras. 19 and 35.

as including the taking of minutes at parish or community meetings and, of course, for his pay to allow for this duty. If the clerk does not take the minutes, they should be taken by the chairman of the parish meeting or, under his direction, by some elector present at the meeting.

Every question is decided by the majority of those present and voting on the question. Each local government elector has the right to give one vote and no more on any question.[1] The decision announced by the chairman is final, unless a poll is demanded. (*See* "Polls".)

As to the expenses of a parish meeting or of the taking of a poll, *see* "Expenses and Expenditure" and "Polls".

For the powers of parish meetings in respect of the creation and dissolution of parish councils, *see* "Parish Council".

The parish meeting has a general power to discuss parish affairs[2] and pass resolutions thereon. Such resolutions will not bind the parish council. However, if a resolution that the council should provide allotments causes the council to be of the opinion that there is a demand for allotments, then the council has a duty to provide them.[3]

Where parishes are grouped under a common parish council, there must, nevertheless, be a separate parish meeting for every parish so grouped (*see* "Grouping of Parishes").

A parish meeting is not a corporate body nor for most purposes is it a local authority.[4] If there is no parish council its property vests, in the case of English parish meetings, in

---

[1] L.G.A. 1972, Sch. 12, paras. 18 and 34.
[2] L.G.A. 1972, ss. 9 and 27.
[3] S.H.A.A. 1908, s. 23.
[4] L.G.A. 1972, s. 270.

the parish trustees (*see* "Parish Trustees") and, in the case of Welsh community meetings, in the county or county borough council (*see* "Community").

A parish meeting in England where there is no council has some of the powers of a parish council (e.g. to provide allotments, to provide burial facilities, to appoint charity trustees, to maintain closed churchyards). In addition, the district or unitary council has power to confer on a parish meeting any function of a parish council.[1]

Not being a local authority for this purpose, a parish meeting cannot recover VAT on its purchases (*see* "Value Added Tax").

## PARISH OFFICES

**(See Public or Parish Offices)**

## PARISH PROPERTY

**(See Property of Parish Council)**

## PARISH TRUSTEES

The parish trustees consist of the chairman of the parish meeting and an official appointed by the district or unitary council. Together they constitute a corporate body to hold the parish property.[2] They have no power to make any decisions of their own, but must act in accordance with any directions given to them by the parish meeting.[3]

---

[1]  L.G.A. 1972, s. 109.
[2]  L.G.A. 1972, s. 13(3).
[3]  L.G.A. 1972, s. 13(4).

The representative body in Wales was not replaced by community trustees and, accordingly, former parish property is vested in the county or county borough council on trust for the community (*see* "Community").

# PARKING PLACES

**(*See also* Commons—Village Greens)**

Parish councils have a general power to provide parking places for motor cars with the consent of the county or unitary council,[1] and may also, without consent, provide and maintain parking places for bicycles and motor-cycles (including structures for use as parking places, e.g. stands for bicycles) where it appears to them to be necessary to do so for the purpose of relieving or preventing congestion of traffic or preserving local amenities.[2]

For the purpose of providing cycle parks only (or for the provision of means of entrance and egress), the parish council may adopt and by order authorise the use of any part of a road within the parish or community. For the provision of any vehicle parks, it may utilise and adopt any land purchased for the purpose or appropriated as described below.

For the definition of "road", *see* "Roads".

The parish council may appropriate for the purpose of providing a parking place, any part of a recreation ground provided or maintained by it under section 8 of the Local Government Act 1894;[3] or of an open space controlled or maintained by it under the Open Spaces Act 1906, other

---

[1]   L.G.A. 1972, Sch. 19, para. 22.
[2]   R.T.R.A. 1984, s. 57.
[3]   *ibid.*

than a part which has been consecrated as a burial ground, or in which burials have taken place; or of any land provided by it as a playing field or for any other purpose under the Local Government (Miscellaneous Provisions) Act 1976 as amended.

No order under these provisions is to authorise the use of any part of a road so as unreasonably to prevent access to any premises adjoining the road, or the use of the road by any person entitled to use it, or so as to be a nuisance.

Various consents may have to be obtained. These are the same as those provided for several purposes in the Act of 1957 (*see* "Consents, etc. under the Parish Councils Act 1957"). The section also applies the same provisions relating to access to telegraphic lines, sewers, etc. as apply to bus shelters (*see* "Bus Shelters").

The parish council may employ with or without remuneration persons for the superintendence of parking places provided by them. They may make orders (subject to the consent of the county council) as to the use of such parking places, in particular as to the charges to be paid where the parking place is not part of a road.

A parking place which is not part of a road may be let for use as a parking place; but no single letting is to be for more than seven days (except as part of a letting under some other enactment of the land of which the parking place forms part).

The exercise of these powers does not render the parish council liable in respect of loss or damage to any vehicle parked in a parking place forming part of a road, or to its fittings or contents.

A parish council may contribute towards the reasonable

expenses incurred by any person in providing a parking place, and towards the expenses of any other parish council in exercising these powers; and may combine with any other parish council for the purpose of exercising these powers.

A parish council may also maintain any parking place which could have been provided by them under this provision, but which was in fact provided, either by them before the commencement of the Act of 1957, or by some other person either before or after the said commencement.

A parish council may prosecute if heavy lorries are parked off a carriageway[1] and the police do not deal with the problem.

## PARKS

### (See Recreation)

## PAROCHIAL CHARITY

### (See Charities)

## PAROCHIAL COMMITTEES

Parochial committees were abolished by the Local Government Act 1972.[2] There is a general power for a county, district or unitary council to delegate any of its functions to a parish council, whereupon the parish council acts as agent.[3]

---

[1] R.T.A. 1988, s. 19.
[2] By not reproducing L.G.A. 1933, s. 87.
[3] L.G.A. 1972, s. 101.

## PASTURE

**(See Common Pasture)**

## PATHS

**(See Footpaths—Footways)**

## PECUNIARY INTERESTS

**(See Interest in Contract or Other Matters)**

## PENSIONS FOR PAID OFFICERS

**(See Superannuation of Paid Officers)**

## PETTY CASH

**(See Accounts)**

## PHYSICAL TRAINING AND RECREATION, PROVISION FOR

**(See Recreation)**

## PLANNING

**(See *also* Untidy Land)**

Generally speaking, under the Town and Country Planning Act 1990, as amended by the Planning and Compensation Act 1991, the Planning and Compulsory Purchase Act 2004 and the Planning Act 2008, any development of land requires the prior permission of the planning authority.

The county council is the planning authority for the county and the district council is the planning authority for the district. This apparently complicated statement is the result of the fact that certain planning powers are allocated to the county and some to the district, whilst others are concurrent powers exercisable by both. In most cases, however, planning applications are the responsibility of the district council. There is a right of appeal by an applicant to the Secretary of State against a refusal of permission to develop. If the parish falls within the area of a unitary authority (whether that be a county council, district council or London borough council), then that authority will be the planning authority.

The relevant planning authority is required to notify the parish council if the parish council informs that authority that it wishes to be notified of planning applications.[1] The authority is obliged to have regard to any comments made by the parish council, provided that they are made within 14 days of the notification. If it is not possible to submit comments within this time limit, they should still be sent nevertheless, because there is no reason why the planning authority should not consider them, although after the time limit they are not obliged to do so. The planning authority is also required to inform the parish council of the result of the application or, if appropriate, of the date when the application was referred to the Secretary of State.[2] (On appeals, *see* "Public Inquiries".) An increasing number of planning authorities are now sending copies of plans to the parish councils in order to enable the parish councils to comprehend the likely effect of applications more readily and thus, in turn, to produce more informed and balanced comments from the parish councils.

---

[1] T.C.P.A. 1990, Sch. 1, para. 8 (England), Sch. 1A, para. 2 (Wales).
[2] Town and Country Planning (General Development Procedure) Order 1995, S.I. 419, Art. 13.

Broadly speaking, "development" includes any building operation other than the maintenance or internal alteration of an existing building; and any material change in the use of any buildings or land, subject to certain exemptions.

A "blanket" permission has been given by the Secretary of State to development of certain specified classes, subject to certain conditions, by the Town and Country Planning (General Permitted Development) Order 1995 (as amended).[1] For development within the scope of the Order, no separate application for permission is necessary. The classes of development covered by it include the erection by parish councils of certain "small ancillary buildings", which it is understood include lamp-posts, litter bins, bus shelters and roadside seats and shelters.

## PLAYGROUNDS AND PLAYING FIELDS

**(See Recreation—Village Greens)**

## PLEASURE GROUNDS

**(See Recreation)**

## PLOUGHING OF PATHS

**(See Footpaths)**

## POLLS

At a parish meeting, every question is decided in the first instance by the majority of those present and voting on the

---

[1] S.I. 418.

question, and the decision of the person presiding at the meeting as to the result of the voting is final, unless a poll is demanded.[1]

A poll may be demanded at any time before the conclusion of a parish meeting.[2]

A poll, however, shall not be taken unless either the chairman of the meeting consents, or the poll is demanded by local government electors present at the meeting, not being less than ten in number or one-third of those present, whichever number is the less. The poll shall be taken on such day as shall be fixed by the returning officer, being a day not earlier than the fourteenth day or, unless for special reasons the Secretary of State otherwise directs, later than the twenty-fifth day after the day on which the poll was demanded.

Every poll consequent on a parish meeting is to be taken by ballot, in accordance with the Parish and Community Meetings (Polls) Rules 1987 as amended.[3]

The expenses of taking a poll are paid by the parish council.

As to the polls at the election of parish councillors, *see* "Election and Appointment of Parish Councillors". As to polls relating to the creation, dissolution and grouping of community councils and communities, *see* "Parish Council – Creation and dissolution of community council in Wales *and* Grouping of parishes – Wales".

---

[1] L.G.A. 1972, Sch. 12, paras. 18(2) and 34(2).

[2] *ibid.*, paras. 18(4) and 34(4).

[3] 1987, S.I. 1, as amended by 1987, S.I. 262 and by the Civil Partnership Act 2004 (Amendments to Subordinate Legislation) Order 2005 (S.I. 2114).

## POLLUTION

**(See Nuisances and Pollution)**

## PONDS

**(See Ditches and Drains)**

## POOLS, SWIMMING

**(See Baths, etc.)**

## POST-MORTEM ROOM

**(See Mortuaries and Post-Mortem Rooms)**

## PRECEPTS

**(See Expenses and Expenditure)**

## PRESERVATION OF TREES AND BUILDINGS

A parish council has no direct powers in these matters but may well wish to take an active interest in them. Both district and county councils have powers in respect of trees and buildings under the Planning Acts.

## PRESS, ADMISSION OF, TO COUNCIL MEETINGS

**(See Meetings of Parish Council)**

# PROCEEDINGS

**(See Legal Proceedings—Parish Council—Parish Meeting—Public Inquiries)**

## PROMOTION OF WELL-BEING

Part 4 of the Local Government and Public Involvement in Health Act 2007 extends to "eligible" parish councils in England the power to promote well-being conferred on principal councils by section 1 of the Local Government Act 2000. A council is eligible if (a) it has a qualified clerk with one (or more) of the certificates granted by the University of Gloucestershire who has had training in the use of the power, (b) at least two-thirds of the vacancies on the council were filled at the last ordinary election, (c) 80 per cent of the councillors have been trained in the use of the power, and (d) the council has published a statement of intent as to community engagement. The Secretary of State has issued guidance on the exercise of the power (see www.communities.gov.uk/publications/localgovernment/powertopromote).

## PROPERTY OF PARISH COUNCIL

**(See *also* Allotments—Community Centres— Compulsory Purchase—Damage—Information about Land—Public or Parish Offices—Recreation— Village Greens—Village Halls)**

### General

Parish property includes old parish workhouses and cottages provided by the overseers before the establishment of boards of guardians under the Poor Law Amendment Act 1834; lands acquired for the employment of the poor;

vestry rooms; parochial offices; land allotted under an inclosure award to be used as village greens, recreation grounds, field gardens, or otherwise for the benefit of the inhabitants. Property formerly held by the board of guardians was transferred to the parish council by section 115 of the Local Government Act 1929.

The legal interest in all property which was formerly vested either in the overseers or in the churchwardens and overseers of the parish, other than property connected with the affairs of the church or held for an ecclesiastical charity, is vested in the parish council, subject to all trusts and liabilities affecting the same.[1]

All buildings, lands and hereditaments purchased, hired or taken on lease under the Poor Relief Act 1819, for the purpose of a workhouse or for the employment of the poor, and also other buildings, lands and hereditaments belonging to the parish are, therefore, vested in the parish council.

It should be observed, however, that the legal interest only is transferred to the council. The net income arising from the property should therefore be applied in accordance with the trusts upon which the property is held and, if it is applicable in aid of the rates, should be paid over to the council responsible for the collection of local government taxes.

### Gifts

A parish council may accept, hold and administer any gift of property (other than a gift for an ecclesiastical charity, or a charity for the relief of the poor) for the purpose of discharging any of its functions, or for the benefit of the

---

[1] L.G.A. 1894, s. 6.

inhabitants of its parish, or of some part of it, and may execute any works (including works of maintenance or improvement) incidental to or consequential on these powers.[1]

Where such works are executed in connection with a gift for the benefit of the inhabitants of the local area (as contrasted with a gift directly related to one of the parish council's statutory powers, e.g. recreation), the cost of the works must come from the free resource (*see* "Free Resource") or, in the case of an "eligible" parish council in England, may be covered by the power of the promotion of well-being (*see* "Promotion of Well-Being").

As to the power of parish councils to provide suitable buildings for council business and public meetings, *see* "Public or Parish Offices".

### Acquisition

A parish council may, by agreement, acquire by way of purchase, lease or exchange, any land, whether within or without its area, for the purpose of any of its functions under any public general Act of Parliament, or for the benefit, improvement or development of its area.[2] It may borrow money for purchasing any land which it is authorised to purchase. (*See* "Loans to Parish Council".) Where land is acquired, it is to be conveyed to the parish council as a corporate body.

As to compulsory purchase, *see* "Compulsory Purchase of Land."

A parish council is authorised to execute any works (including works of maintenance or improvement) in

---

[1]  L.G.A. 1972, s. 139.
[2]  L.G.A. 1972, s. 124.

relation to any acquired land but, if the land was acquired for the benefit, etc. of its area, expenditure on works is limited to the free resource (*see* "Free Resource") or, in the case of an "eligible" parish council in England, may be covered by the power of well-being (*see* "Promotion of Well-Being"). If, on the other hand, the land was acquired specifically for a statutory function, e.g. a playing field, there is no limit on the amount which may be spent.

A piece of land acquired for a specific purpose but not immediately required for that purpose, may be used temporarily for another purpose, so long as such use does not interfere with its use in due course for the purpose for which the land was acquired. It is not essential that during this time the land should be kept in the state which it was in when it was acquired.

## Appropriation

Any land belonging to a parish council which is not required for the purpose for which it was acquired, or which has since been appropriated, may be appropriated for any other purpose for which the council is authorised to acquire land by agreement.[1] There are procedural restrictions on appropriating common land and open spaces but, if these are satisfied, any public trust in the land ceases.

The consent of the Secretary of State is not required for appropriation except in the case of common land (which includes a town or village green) in excess of 250 square yards.

Appropriation may involve some adjustment in the accounts.

---

[1] L.G.A. 1972, s. 126, as amended by L.G.P.L.A. 1980, Sch. 23, paras. 17 and 18.

## Letting

A parish council may let any land vested in it whether or not it is held for charitable purposes.[1] However, unless the lease is for seven years or less, the rent must be the best which can reasonably be obtained. If this is not so, the consent of the Secretary of State is required.[2] Land includes buildings and the parish council thus has power to let any building vested in it.

## Disposal

A parish council may sell any land it possesses. No Ministerial consent is required except that if land is sold for a consideration less than the best which can reasonably be obtained, the consent of the Secretary of State is necessary.[3] There are also certain restrictions on the disposition of charity land.[4] Capital money arising in cases other than the disposal of charity land may only be applied towards the discharge of debt or otherwise for capital purposes with the consent of the Secretary of State.[5]

Public trust land must not be sold unless the council gives notice in the local newspaper in two successive weeks and considers any objections which may be made to it. If such land is sold, it is freed from any trust arising solely because

---

[1]  Ch.A. 1993, ss. 36 and 37.
[2]  L.G.A. 1972, s. 127. The details are contained in C.L.G. Circular 06/03: *Local Government Act 1972 general disposal consent (England) 2003 – disposal of land for less than the best consideration that can be reasonably be obtained* and in N.A.F.W.C. 41/03: *Local Government Act 1972 – general disposal consent (Wales) 2003.* Consent is given by the circulars to disposals which promote or improve the economic, social or environmental well-being of the relevant council's area so long as the difference between the unrestricted value of the land and the consideration for disposal does not exceed £2 million.
[3]  L.G.A. 1972, s. 127.
[4]  Ch.A. 1993, ss. 36 and 37.
[5]  L.G.A. 1972, s. 153.

it is public trust land.[1]

Where, however, land has been purchased specifically for allotments, it is provided by the Allotments Act of 1925 that the parish council shall not sell, appropriate, use or dispose of the land for any other purpose without the consent of the Secretary of State (*see* "Allotments").

Parish councils are exempt from capital gains tax.

## Protection of property

The parish council may incur expense in prosecuting or defending legal proceedings for the protection of property vested in it. For planning inquiries affecting such property, *see* "Public Inquiries".

If another local authority seeks to acquire compulsorily the property of a parish council and the council's objection is not withdrawn, the acquisition may, in certain circumstances, be subject to special parliamentary procedure, as provided by the Acquisition of Land Act 1981. The Statutory Orders (Special Procedure) Acts 1945 and 1965 then apply. In brief, the proposal is examined at a local inquiry at which the parish council can state its case. It may further petition against the order which is then examined by a Joint Committee of both Houses of Parliament, at which the parish council can, if necessary, be represented by counsel. The costs of such representation may, of course, be substantial and the council would no doubt wish to take advice before incurring them.

Parish property, other than commons, village greens and recreation grounds irrevocably dedicated to the public, is liable to be rated for local non-domestic rates. (*See* "Rating

---

[1] L.G.A. 1972, s. 127(3), as substituted by L.G.P.L.A. 1980, Sch. 23, para. 19.

and Valuation".) Income received by a parish council arising from parish property is exempt from income tax and corporation tax.

## PROSECUTIONS BY PARISH COUNCIL
### (*See* Legal Proceedings)

## PUBLIC, ADMISSION OF, TO COUNCIL MEETINGS
### (*See* Meetings of Parish Council)

## PUBLIC BATHING, REGULATION OF
### (*See* By-laws)

## PUBLIC CLOCKS

A parish council is empowered to provide, maintain and light public clocks within the parish and to install them on or against any premises or in any other convenient situation.[1]

The exercise of this power is subject to provisions as to consents and access to telegraphic lines, etc.[2] (*See* "Consents, etc. under the Parish Councils Act 1957".)

A parish council may maintain a public clock provided by it before the commencement of the Act, or provided by any other person whether before or after such commencement; and may contribute towards the reasonable expenses of any other person, or the expenses of any other council, in the

---

[1] P.C.A. 1957, s. 2.
[2] As set out in P.C.A. 1957, s. 5.

provision or maintenance of a public clock. An example is a church clock.

## PUBLIC CONVENIENCES

A parish council has the power to provide public conveniences, provided that it does not place them in or under a highway or proposed highway without the consent of the highway authority, or district council if the latter is maintaining the highway.[1]

In providing such conveniences, the council has a duty to make provision, so far as is practical and reasonable, for the needs of disabled persons, and to display appropriate notices.[2]

## PUBLIC GIFTS
### (See Property of Parish Council)

## PUBLIC HEALTH
### (See Ditches and Drains—Limits upon the Powers of the Parish Council)

## PUBLIC INFORMATION
### (See Information for the Public)

## PUBLIC INQUIRIES

Many public inquiries, especially those into planning applications, are of considerable interest to a parish

---

[1] P.H.A. 1936, s. 87.
[2] Chronically Sick and Disabled Persons Act 1970, ss. 5, 7.

as a whole, and the parish council may wish to make representations in such cases. If they are taking a similar view to the county council or the district council, the best course may be for the chairman or clerk of the parish council to be called as a witness by whoever is presenting the other authority's case but, on occasion, the parish council may wish to represent its views separately, either because it takes a different view from the larger authority or for some other reason.

Planning appeals are normally concerned with questions of fact rather than law, and there is no rule that persons appearing at public inquiries must be legally represented. There are, however, cases where, for one reason or another, the parish council may consider that legal representation is desirable. Where the parish council's own property is affected, or the inquiry concerns the parish council as an authority, the council has an inherent right to incur necessary expenditure to defend its interests but, in all cases, the council has a statutory power to incur expenditure in appearing and representing its inhabitants at any public or other inquiry held by any ministry or public body under any Act.[1]

## PUBLIC NOTICES

### (See Notices)

## PUBLIC OR PARISH OFFICES

### (See *also* Property of Parish Council—Rooms in School and Rooms Maintained Out of Rates)

In many of the larger parishes, vestry rooms or offices for the transaction of parochial business were acquired or erected

---

[1] L.G.A. 1972, s. 222.

by the overseers. Where such rooms or offices existed before the Local Government Act 1894 came into force, the legal interest in them passed to the parish council.

The powers of overseers to provide a vestry room or parochial room were transferred by the Local Government Act 1894 to the parish council. These powers are no longer required, as a parish council has a general power, without sanction from any government department (unless a loan is required), to provide or acquire and furnish buildings for transacting the business of the council, or of the parish meeting, or any other parish business,[1] and for public meetings and assemblies, or to contribute towards the expenses incurred by any other parish council or any other person in providing or acquiring and furnishing such a building.[2] The parish council may also move the district or unitary council to acquire compulsorily land for the purpose of providing or acquiring such buildings. (*See* "Compulsory Purchase of Land".)

Parish offices may be used by the council for entertainments, lectures, etc., or may be let to any person for the same purpose. Former restrictions on such use have been lifted. (*See* "Recreation".) The receipts from the occasional letting of a room for concerts, etc. should be entered in the accounts of the parish council.

A council may borrow money for the purchase of land or any building which the council is authorised to purchase or erect. (*See* "Loans to Parish Council".)

## PUBLIC PATHS

### (See Footpaths)

---

[1]  L.G.A. 1972, s. 111.
[2]  L.G.A. 1972, s. 133.

## PUBLIC RIGHTS OF WAY

**(See Highways)**

## PUBLIC SERVICES OMBUDSMAN FOR WALES

**(See Commission for Local Administration)**

## PUBLIC WALKS

**(See Recreation)**

## PUBLIC WORKS LOANS BOARD

**(See Loans to Parish Council)**

## PUMPS

**(See Water Supply)**

## QUALIFICATIONS FOR ELECTORS

**(See Local Government Electors)**

## QUALIFICATIONS FOR OFFICE OF PARISH COUNCILLOR

**(See Parish Councillor)**

## QUALITY PARISH COUNCILS

The quality parish councils scheme was launched in March 2003. The main points of the scheme are, in summary, as follows.

**The quality criteria**

In order to attain quality parish status, a parish council must demonstrate that it has the attributes expected of a quality parish council and has the ability and capacity to take on the enhanced role and responsibility that quality status will bring. Tests have been devised to measure these criteria and cover the following:–

*Test 1 – Electoral mandate*

On first accreditation only: at least 80% of all council seats were filled at the beginning of the current four-year term by members who stood for election at that time.

On re-accreditation: all council seats are filled at the beginning of the current four-year term by members who stood for election at that time. This does not mean that there must be a ballot/election. "Stood for election" for the purposes of the quality scheme means councillors must have been nominated and stood as candidates. Where the number of candidates is the same as (or less than) the number of seats, then no ballot is held and candidates are automatically declared "elected" by the returning officer. In such cases, at least 80% of councillors must have been nominated and prepared to stand at the last round of elections in order to pass this test.

*Test 2 – Qualifications of the clerk*

The clerk to the council must hold one of the following qualifications:–

(a) Certificate in Local Council Administration; or

(b) Certificate of Higher Education in Local Policy or Local Council Administration awarded by the University of Gloucestershire.

The council should ensure that appropriate training and support is available to the clerk in order to help meet this test.

## Test 3 – Council meetings

The council must meet on at least six occasions every year (the annual parish meeting may be counted as one of the meetings). Notices of the meeting must be publicly displayed at least three days before each meeting. Minutes of meetings must be available for inspection by electors. Time must be allowed at each meeting for public participation.

## Test 4 – Effective communication

There are mandatory and discretionary elements to this Test. The mandatory requirements are as follows:–

Publication of regular information, perhaps in the form of a newsletter at least four times a year, including information on councillors and how they can be contacted, and a synopsis of the annual report. Information must be readily available at public sites across the parish. In addition, councils must meet at least nine of the discretionary requirements.

The discretionary elements comprise activities such as sending newsletters/annual reports to each household, maintenance of a parish council website, e-mail facilities, councillors' surgeries and consultation exercises.

## Test 5 – Annual report

Publication of an annual report, including certain information, within a prescribed timescale and made readily available at sites across the parish.

## Test 6 – Accountability

Accounts prepared in accordance with the requirements of the Accounts and Audit Regulations; unqualified accounts; adequate systems of internal control.

*Test 7 – Ethical framework*

Adoption of a local code of conduct (*see* Appendices 1 and 2).

## The accreditation process

Applications for quality parish status are vetted by panels at county level, established by the National Association of Local Councils (N.A.L.C.) in consultation with stakeholders, including the Local Government Association and the Society of Local Council Clerks and approved by C.L.G. and D.E.F.R.A. N.A.L.C.'s county associations service the panels.

C.L.G. and D.E.F.R.A. approve a panel's membership where they are satisfied that the panel collectively have experience and knowledge of both principal local authorities and parish councils.

Where the panel decline to confer quality parish status, the council is told why and the panel indicates the specific improvements that are expected and a date after which it will be possible to apply again for quality parish status.

Successful parish councils receive a certificate confirming their quality parish status for four years and are able to use the quality parish council logo during this period. Parish councils are required to re-apply every four years to keep their quality parish status.

A fee is charged to cover the costs of the accreditation process.

The scheme does not apply in Wales. The National Assembly commissioned a study of the powers and functions of community councils which reported in August 2003 with a recommendation to introduce an accreditation scheme for community councils on the lines of the quality parish councils scheme. The Assembly did not adopt the recommendation.

## QUORUM

There is no rule which provides for a quorum at a parish meeting. In the case of a parish council, the quorum is one third of the total number of members of the council, but with the qualification that in no event must the quorum be less than three.[1] If, for some reason, more than one third of the members of the council are disqualified at the same time, the quorum is to be calculated by taking one third of the number of members remaining qualified, again with the qualification that there is a minimum of three.[2]

## RATING AND VALUATION

Parish councils have no responsibility either for valuation or for the collection of rates or other local taxes.

In most cases, the district or unitary council is the responsible authority for raising local taxes, including rates on non-domestic property (see Local Government Finance Act 1988). If there is any income for the benefit of the parish paid to the district or unitary council, it reduces the overall charge levied in the parish.

Agricultural land and agricultural buildings are exempted from rates. Agricultural land includes allotments and allotment gardens.

Also exempt are parks, recreation grounds, open spaces, etc. provided by, or under the management of, a local authority

---

[1] L.G.A. 1972, Sch. 12, paras. 12 and 28.
[2] *ibid.*, para. 45.

(which includes a parish council or parish meeting) and available for use by members of the public.

Parish councils will doubtless assure themselves that the valuation list exempts property of these kinds in which they are interested. They may also be concerned with the eligibility for rate relief of certain property. There is mandatory relief for 80% of the full rates on property occupied by a charity and wholly or mainly used for charitable purposes; and rating authorities have discretionary power to allow further relief of up to 100% for a range of organisations including sports clubs. Although these measures do not normally extend to property occupied by parish councils, relief is permissible if the council is occupying the property as trustees.

Domestic property is subject to council tax, not to non-domestic rates (*see* "Council Tax"). Parish councils cannot precept on non-domestic rates.

# READING AND RECREATION ROOMS

**(See Public or Parish Offices)**

# RECORDS

**(See Books and Documents)**

# RECREATION

**(See *also* By-laws—Commons—Community Centres—Expenses—Open Spaces—Roadside Seats and Shelters—Swimming Pools—Tourism—Village Greens)**

### Pleasure grounds, parks and public walks

A parish council has power to acquire land for a pleasure ground, park or a public walk. It may purchase or take on lease, lay out, plant, improve and maintain lands for these purposes and may maintain or contribute to the maintenance of these facilities provided by any person.[1] The council may make by-laws for the regulation of any such land which is under its control, or to the expense of which it has contributed. Any by-laws must be confirmed by the Secretary of State. The council may, on such days as it thinks fit (not exceeding 12 days in any one year, or six consecutive days on one occasion) close any such land or part thereof to the public and may grant the use of it, either free or for payment, to any public charity or institution, or for any agricultural, horticultural or other show or other public purpose, or may use the ground itself for any such show or purpose. Not more than one quarter of the total available public pleasure land may, however, be closed on any Sunday or public holiday. The admission to the ground on any closed day may be either with or without payment.[2]

The council may either itself provide and let for hire, or license any person to let for hire, any pleasure boats on any lake or piece of water in any such pleasure ground and may make by-laws regulating the same. It may also provide a boating pool, the boats and any equipment reasonably required for this purpose.[3]

## Playing fields, recreational facilities and centres

A parish council is empowered to provide inside or outside its area such recreational facilities as it thinks fit, including the provision of buildings, equipment, supplies and assistance of any kind. These powers are very wide and cover all kinds of indoor and outdoor recreations,

---

[1] P.H.A. 1875, s. 164, and L.G.A. 1972, Sch. 14, para. 27.
[2] P.H.A.A.A. 1890, s. 44, and P.H.A. 1961, s. 53.
[3] P.H.A. 1961, s. 54.

e.g. tennis courts, squash courts, swimming pools,[1] etc. The facilities may be provided free or for such charges as the council considers appropriate.[2] The facilities may be let to voluntary organisations.[3] The Secretary of State may make grants to voluntary organisations towards capital expenditure under the Act for purposes of physical training and recreation. Parish councils may obtain grants from county or district councils or from Fields in Trust (formerly the National Playing Fields Association), Ground Floor South, 100 Christian Street, London E1 1RS (www.fieldsintrust.org.uk). Another useful contact is Sport England, 3rd Floor, Victoria House, Bloomsbury Square, London WC1B 4SE (www.sportengland.org.uk). The address of the Sports Council for Wales is National Sports Centre, Sophia Gardens, Cardiff CF1 9SW (www. sports-council-wales.co.uk). (*See* "Grants".)

Premises provided for recreational purposes may be used by the parish council for concerts or other entertainments which may be provided by the council or by any other person; and they may be let for these purposes, or for meetings.

The county council and the district council have concurrent powers for the same purpose; and a parish council may contribute (either by way of grant or loan) towards the expenses incurred by another local authority, or by a voluntary organisation, in providing or maintaining any facility which the parish council may provide. Similarly, another local authority may contribute to the expenses of the parish council.

---

[1] As to swimming pools, *see* "Baths, Wash-houses, Swimming Pools and Bathing Places".

[2] L.G.(M.P.)A. 1976, s. 19.

[3] L.G.A. 1972, s. 127. The Secretary of State gave a general consent for such lettings in January 1977.

For powers to acquire land compulsorily, *see* "Compulsory Purchase of Land".

A recreation ground which is irrevocably dedicated to the public is not rateable, provided that on the actual facts of the case it can be shown that the public is the true occupier. As to the rating of playing fields, *see* "Rating and Valuation".

## REFUSE
**(See Litter)**

## REORGANISATION OF PARISHES
**(See Alteration of Areas—Grouping of Parishes)**

## REPRESENTATIVE BODY
**(See Parish Trustees)**

## RESIGNATION
**(See Chairman of Parish Council—Parish Councillor)**

## RESOLUTION
**(See Meetings of Parish Council)**

## RESPONSIBLE FINANCIAL OFFICER
**(See Accounts—Treasurer of Parish Council)**

## RETIREMENT FROM OFFICE
**(See Parish Councillor)**

# REVIEW OF BOUNDARIES

**(See Alteration of Areas)**

# RIGHTS OF WAY

**(See Footpaths—Highways)**

# ROADS

**(See *also* Consents, etc. under the Parish Councils Act 1957—Ditches and Drains—Highways—Lighting— Parking Places—Roadside Seats and Shelters— Roadside Waste)**

For the purposes of the provisions of the Parish Councils Act 1957 and the Road Traffic Regulation Act 1984, relating to lighting, parking places and seats and shelters in roads, "road" is defined[1] as meaning any highway (including a public path) and any other road, lane, footway, square, court, alley or passage (whether a thoroughfare or not) to which the public has access, but does not include a special road (as defined by the Highways Act 1980).[2]

# ROADSIDE DITCHES

**(See Ditches and Drains)**

# ROADSIDE SALES

**(See Highways)**

---

[1] P.C.A. 1957, s. 7, and R.T.R.A. 1984, s. 60(4).
[2] H.A. 1980, s. 16.

# ROADSIDE SEATS AND SHELTERS
## (*See also* Bus Shelters)

A parish council may provide and maintain seats and shelters for the use of the public and install or erect them in proper and convenient situations in, or on any land abutting on, any road within the parish.[1]

For the definition of "road", *see* "Roads".

The exercise of the powers is subject to various consents[2] (*see* "Consents, etc. under the Parish Councils Act 1957"), and to the same provisions relating to access to telegraphic lines, sewers, etc. as apply to bus shelters (*see* "Bus Shelters").

A parish council may combine with any other parish council for the joint exercise of these powers;[3] may contribute towards the expenses of any parish council in the exercise of the powers;[4] and may contribute towards the reasonable expenses of any person in doing anything which the council is empowered to do under these provisions.[5]

The parish council may also maintain any seat or shelter which could have been provided by it under these provisions but was in fact provided either by it before the commencement of the Act or by some other person either before or after the said commencement.[6]

As to borrowing for this purpose, *see* "Loans to Parish Council".

---

[1] P.C.A. 1957, s. 1.
[2] P.C.A. 1957, s. 5.
[3] L.G.A. 1972, s. 101(5).
[4] P.C.A. 1957, s. 6(1).
[5] *ibid.*
[6] P.C.A. 1957, s. 6(2).

Planning permission is not required for the provision of seats and shelters (*see* "Planning").

## ROADSIDE VERGES

### (See Highways—Roadside Wastes)

## ROADSIDE WASTES

Where on either side of a public road strips of land exist open to the public, between the metalled road and the fences beyond, *prima facie* the public right of way extends, unless there is evidence to the contrary, over such strips of roadside wastes, and they cannot lawfully be enclosed by the owner of the adjoining land, or by the lord of the manor, or by any other person.

Such strips may be of varying width, and the adjoining owner has no right to straighten the line of his fences by taking in any part of the roadside waste. The public, in the absence of proof to the contrary, have the right to the whole of the roadside waste between the fences and the metalled road. The fact that trees or shrubs have been allowed to grow upon these roadside wastes so as to interfere with their use by the public does not destroy such right or justify the enclosure of any such wastes.

A parish council which considers that a roadside waste has been unlawfully encroached upon, may make representations on the subject to the district or unitary council which then has a duty to take proceedings on the matter, unless satisfied that the allegations are incorrect.[1] Roadside waste was not registrable under the Commons

---

[1]   H.A. 1980, s. 130.

Registration Act 1965 and is not registrable under the Commons Act 2006.

In certain cases the courts have held that a parish council has a right to let the herbage on the roadside wastes.[1] The right must be established by evidence of ancient custom or grant under a parish award or otherwise.

## ROOMS IN SCHOOL AND ROOMS MAINTAINED OUT OF RATES

### (See *also* Meetings of Parish Council—Public or Parish Offices)

Where there is no suitable public room vested in the parish council or parish trustees which can be used free of charge, a suitable room in a school maintained by a local education authority, or a suitable room, the expense of maintaining which is payable out of any rate, may be used free of charge at all reasonable times and after reasonable notice for any of the following purposes:–

(a) a parish meeting or any meeting of the parish council; or

(b) meetings convened by the chairman of the parish meeting in England or by the parish council; or

(c) the administration of public funds within or for the purposes of the parish where these funds are administered by any committee or officer appointed, either by the parish meeting or by the parish council or by a county or district council.[2]

---

[1] A.G. *v. Garner* [1907] 2 K.B. 480.
[2] L.G.A. 1972, s. 134.

194

The use of any room used as part of a private dwelling-house such, for instance, as the teacher's residence, is, however, not authorised.

The school hours of a day or evening school must not be interfered with. Care should be taken to select a time which will cause the least possible inconvenience to the persons responsible for the conduct of the school.

The freedom from charge relates to expenses in the nature of rent. It does not necessarily extend to freedom from charge for services rendered in connection with the use of the room, such as heating, lighting or cleaning or, as indicated below, the repair of damage.

In the case of a room used for the purposes of the administration of justice, or for the purposes of the police, there must be no interference with the hours during which the room is used for those purposes.

If any question arises as to what is "reasonable" or "suitable", it is to be determined, in the case of a school room, by the Secretary of State; in the case of a room used for the purposes of the administration of justice, or for the purposes of the police, by the Home Secretary; and in any other case, by the Secretary of State.

As to what is "reasonable notice", the Secretary of State advises that (except as regards some meetings of parish councils) the notice should be served not less than seven clear days before the date named and that, in most cases, longer notice, as a rule not less than 14 days' notice, should be given. As regards meetings of parish councils, three clear days' notice would ordinarily suffice for a special parish council meeting but longer notice should, if possible, be given.

Any expense incurred for damage or otherwise in connection with the use of the room must be defrayed, in the case of an inquiry as part of the expenses of the inquiry, and in any other case as expenses of the parish meeting or parish council.

A candidate at an election of a parish councillor is entitled, for the purpose of holding public meetings in furtherance of his candidature, to the use free of charge at reasonable times between the last day on which notice of the election may be published and the day preceding the day of election, of a suitable room in the premises of a community, foundation or voluntary school situated in the electoral area for which he is a candidate (or if there is no such school in that area in any such school in an adjacent electoral area) or in a parish or community in part comprised in that electoral area.[1]

He may also use any meeting room situated in the electoral area for which he is standing or in a parish or community in part comprised in that electoral area, the expense of maintaining which is payable wholly or mainly out of public funds or out of any rate, or by a body whose expenses are so payable. Here again, this provision does not authorise the use of a room used as part of a private dwelling-house, or any interference with the hours during which the school-house is used for educational purposes. Any expense incurred for damage or otherwise in connection with the use of the room must be defrayed by the person by whom, or on whose behalf, the meeting was convened.

Any question arising in connection with the above provision as to what is "reasonable" or "suitable" is to be determined by the Secretary of State.

---

[1]  R.P.A. 1983, s. 96, as substituted by R.P.A. 1985, Sch. 5, as amended by the School Standards and Framework Act 1998, Sch. 30, para. 11.

# SALE
*(See Property of Parish Council)*

# SCHOOL GOVERNORS
*(See Education)*

# SCHOOL ROOM
*(See Rooms in School, etc.)*

# SEAL
*(See Parish Council)*

# SEATS
*(See Roadside Seats and Shelters)*

# SECTION 137 OF THE L.G.A. 1972
*(See Free Resource)*

# SECURITY OF OFFICERS
*(See Insurance—Treasurer of Parish Council)*

# SHELTERS
*(See Bus Shelters—Roadside Seats and Shelters)*

# SIGNS AND SIGNPOSTS
*(See Highways—Footpaths)*

## SPECIAL EXPENSES

**(See Expenses and Expenditure)**

## SPRING

**(See Water Supply)**

## STANDARDS BOARD

**(See *also* Monitoring Officer—Standards Committee)**

The Standards Board for England is responsible for monitoring ethical standards in local government in England. It has powers to investigate complaints against councillors for breach of a council's code of conduct (*see* "Code of Conduct") and to impose sanctions if a breach is found. Sanctions include suspension and disqualification from office. The Board's address is Fourth Floor, Griffin House, 40 Lever Street, Manchester M1 1BB (www.standardsforengland.gov.uk).

These functions are performed in Wales by the Public Services Ombudsman for Wales (*see* "Commission for Local Administration").

## STANDARDS COMMITTEE

Every principal council is required to have a standards committee or sub-committee for the parish councils in its area, the functions of which include the maintenance of high standards of conduct among councillors and giving assistance to them in observing the council's code of conduct (*see* "Code of Conduct").[1] The committee or sub-

---

[1] L.G.A. 2000, s. 55 (England); s. 56 (Wales).

committee must have at least one parish council member and, generally speaking, a parish councillor member of the committee or sub-committee must be present when matters relating to a parish council are discussed.

# STANDING ORDERS

## (See *also* Contracts of Parish Council)

A council may make standing orders for the regulation of its proceedings and business and may vary or revoke any such orders.[1] A parish council in England may make, vary and revoke such orders for the regulation of proceedings and business of the parish meeting.[2] A parish council may also make standing orders to regulate the quorum, proceedings and place of meeting of any committee of the council, and (in conjunction with the other authority or authorities concerned) of any joint committee.[3]

A parish council may also make standing orders with respect to the making of contracts by the council. However, it *must* make such orders with respect to contracts for the supply of goods or materials to the council, or for the carrying out of any works, which orders must include a provision for regulating the manner in which tenders are invited, but may exempt from any such provision contracts below a certain fixed price or, generally, where the council is satisfied that exemption is justified by special circumstances.[4]

Model standing orders are obtainable from the National Association of Local Councils, 109 Great Russell Street, London WC1B 3LD (www.nalc.gov.uk).

---

[1] L.G.A. 1972, Sch. 12, para. 42.
[2] *ibid.*, para. 20.
[3] L.G.A. 1972, s. 106.
[4] L.G.A. 1972, s. 135.

## STATUTORY NUISANCES

**(*See* Noise—Nuisances and Pollution)**

## STILES OR GATES, REPAIR OF

**(*See* Footpaths)**

## STOPPING UP OF A HIGHWAY

**(*See* Highways)**

## STREAM

**(*See* Water Supply)**

## STREET FURNITURE, DAMAGE TO

**(*See* Damage)**

## STREET LIGHTING

**(*See* Lighting)**

## STYLE OF PARISH

**(*See* Name and Style of Parish)**

## SUBSCRIPTIONS TO ASSOCIATIONS

There is a specific power for a parish council to pay a reasonable subscription to the funds of any association of local authorities formed (whether inside or outside the

United Kingdom) for the purpose of consultation as to the common interest of those authorities and the discussion of matters relating to local government. The parish council may also pay subscriptions to the funds of any associations of members or officers of local authorities formed for the like purposes.[1]

Subscriptions to associations other than local government associations may be paid out of the free resource (*see* "Free Resource").

## SUBSISTENCE ALLOWANCES

### (See Allowances to Parish Councillors)

## SUCCESSOR COUNCIL

### (See Parish Council)

## SUPERANNUATION OF PAID OFFICERS

In those cases in which the salary paid to an officer of the council is his sole or main source of income and his services are full-time, it may be desirable to make provision for his superannuation. This can be done through the appropriate superannuation fund usually maintained by the county council, by a statutory resolution of the parish council (specifying each officer covered).[2] At least 28 days' public notice must be given of the terms of the resolution and the fact that it will be moved at the meeting.

The broad principle of the statutory scheme is that percentage deductions are currently made from the officer's

[1] L.G.A. 1972, s. 143.
[2] L.G. Pension Scheme Regulations 1995, S.I. 1019, Reg. B1(i).

salary, with corresponding contributions payable by the council, into the superannuation fund. Upon retirement, subject to certain conditions, a pension is payable out of the fund based on the officer's average annual remuneration in his final years of service.

Other benefits which may be obtained include widows' pensions (subject to a reduction of the retirement grant) and death grants.

Where a pension is not payable, a parish council can, at its discretion, award an officer a gratuity upon retirement.[1] This may be a lump sum, or an annuity up to the amount specified under the 1996 Regulations. This charge falls directly upon the council's funds and not upon the superannuation fund. Such a gratuity can be paid to a part-time employee.

The foregoing is no more than a brief sketch. It is subject to various qualifications in respect of the relevant service and the calculation of the amounts.

## SWIMMING POOLS

### (*See* Baths, etc.)

## TAX

### (*See* Income Tax—Value Added Tax)

## TERM OF OFFICE OF PARISH COUNCILLORS

### (*See* Election and Appointment of Parish Councillors)

---

[1] L.G. (Discretionary Payment) Regulations 1996, S.I. 1680.

## THIRD PARTY RISKS

### (See Insurance)

## TITHE APPORTIONMENT AND MAP

### (See Books and Documents)

## TOMBSTONES

### (See Burial and Cremation)

## TOURISM

### (See *also* Recreation)

A parish council has power to encourage persons to visit its area, by advertisement or otherwise, for recreation, health purposes, conferences, trade fairs and exhibitions. It may provide, or encourage other persons or bodies to provide, facilities for conferences, trade fairs and exhibitions. It may also improve, or encourage other persons or bodies to improve, any existing facilities for these purposes.[1]

## TOWN AND COUNTRY PLANNING

### (See Planning)

## TOWN COUNCIL

Any parish council, which is not subject to a grouping order, may itself resolve that the parish will have the status of a

---

[1] L.G.A. 1972, s. 144, as amended by L.G.(M.P.)A. 1976, ss. 19(5), 81(1), and Sch. 2.

town, whereupon the council becomes the town council, the chairman and vice-chairman of the council are entitled to the style of town mayor and deputy town mayor, and the parish meeting becomes the town meeting.[1] Such an arrangement does not require the consent or approval of any other council or of the Secretary of State.

## TOWN MAYOR

### (See Chairman of Parish Council—Town Council)

## TRAFFIC CALMING

### (See Highways)

## TRANSPORT

### Car-sharing schemes

A parish council may establish a car-sharing scheme for the benefit of people in the council's area, or assist others in so doing.[2]

### Grants for bus services

A parish council may make grants to any body which operates bus services for the elderly or disabled, or a community bus service, for the benefit of people in the council's area.[3]

### Taxi fare concessions

A parish council may enter into arrangements with a

---

[1]  L.G.A. 1972, s. 245(6).
[2]  L.G.R.A. 1997, s. 26.
[3]  Transport Act 1985, s. 106A, inserted by L.G.R.A. 1997, s. 27.

licensed taxi operator whereby the council reimburses the operator the cost of running a fare concession scheme for residents in the council's area who are eligible to receive travel concessions.[1]

## Information about transport

A parish council may investigate (a) the provision and use of public passenger transport in its area, (b) the use of and need for roads in its area, and (c) the management and control of traffic in its area. It may also publicise information about public passenger services in its area.[2]

# TRAVEL ALLOWANCES

**(See Allowances to Parish Councillors)**

# TREASURER OF PARISH COUNCIL

**(See *also* Accounts—Deputy Officers—Employees)**

The parish council may appoint one of its members to take the office of treasurer without remuneration,[3] but nowadays it is usual to employ an officer for this purpose.[4] Frequently, the offices of clerk and treasurer are combined. In all cases a parish council must ensure that one of its officers has responsibility for the administration of its financial affairs.[5]

The council must take from its treasurer such security for the faithful execution of his office as the council considers

---

[1] L.G.R.A. 1997, s. 28.
[2] L.G.R.A. 1997, s. 29.
[3] L.G.A. 1972, s. 112(5).
[4] L.G.A. 1972, s. 112(1) and (2).
[5] L.G.A. 1972, s. 151.

sufficient.[1] The parish council must defray the cost of the security. Every such security must be produced at audit.

Every cheque or other order for the payment of money by the parish council must be signed by two members of the council.[2]

Like the clerk of a parish council, the treasurer must disclose any interest which he has in any contract of the council. (*See* "Clerk of Parish Council".)

# TRUSTEES

## (See Charities—Parish Trustees)

# TRUSTEE SECURITIES

## (See Investment)

# UNHEALTHY DWELLINGS

## (See Housing)

# UNTIDY LAND

## (See *also* Information about Land—Litter)

Under the Town and Country Planning Act 1990,[3] a planning authority may serve on the owner of untidy land a notice requiring him to take appropriate steps to tidy up the land. Failure to comply with the notice may result in a fine of up to level 3 on the standard scale for

---

[1] L.G.A. 1972, s. 114.
[2] L.G.A. 1972, s. 150(5).
[3] T.C.P.A. 1990, s. 215.

summary offences (currently £1,000) and to a further fine of up to £40 per day for continued failure to comply after conviction. Furthermore, the planning authority which served the notice may enter the land and itself carry out the necessary work, charging the cost to the owner. There is nothing to prevent parish councils from reporting cases to the planning authority with a request for action to be taken as above.

The Secretary of State has power to make grants for the purpose of reclaiming, improving or bringing into use derelict land.[1]

## VALUATION LISTS

### (See Rating and Valuation)

## VALUE ADDED TAX

Value added tax (V.A.T.) is charged essentially on the supply of goods and services in the United Kingdom and on the importation of goods into the United Kingdom.[2] The administration of the tax is under the control of H.M. Revenue and Customs.

A parish council must register with the appropriate Revenue and Customs Office if it supplies, or expects to supply, any goods or services for which payment is made by the recipient (other than wholly through rates) which fall within the definition of "taxable" supply. A supply of goods or services is a "taxable" supply if it is either standard rated or zero rated.

---

[1]  Derelict Land Act 1982, s. 1.
[2]  Value Added Tax Act 1994, s. 1.

H.M. Revenue and Customs supply notices which should be obtained by any parish council wishing to study the implications of V.A.T. for the activities of the council.[1]

Examples of services which a parish council may supply which might require V.A.T. to be taken into account include matters relating to cemeteries, recreation, entertainments, highways, parking places, etc. Certain activities are, however, exempted.

The basic or standard rate of value added tax is currently 17.5%.[2] This can be changed up or down within certain limits by a Treasury order without parliamentary approval.[3] This standard rate must be charged by a local council on any service or goods supplied. Certain services and goods are zero rated (see leaflet No. 749). The local council must, nevertheless, technically charge value added tax at zero rate on the provision of these services or goods. These charges, i.e. at standard rate or zero rate, are called the output tax and must be clearly shown in the accounts.

Once it has been established that a supply is to be rated for value added tax (whether at standard or zero rate), the local council may then *deduct* any tax which it itself paid, e.g. on purchase of goods before supplying them, or on services rendered to the council in connection with the subsequent supply (i.e. the input tax – also to be clearly shown in the accounts). The balance between the output tax recovered by the local council and the input tax paid is then to be paid to H.M. Revenue and Customs.

In addition, a parish council, whether registered as above or not, is entitled to *recover* any *input* tax paid by the

---

[1] Numbers 749 and 749A.
[2] As from 1st January 2010.
[3] Value Added Tax Act 1994, s. 2.

council in respect of any goods or services acquired by the council for any non-business activity, e.g. the tidying up of grass verges. A registered parish council may do this on form VAT 100 on a monthly basis. A non-registered council should apply periodically to H.M. Revenue and Customs, 2nd Floor, Alexander House, Southend-on-Sea, Essex SS99 1AU.

There are special rules covering supplies of goods and services which are exempt, or partly exempt, from V.A.T. (see V.A.T. Notice 749) and for the disposal or acquisition of land and property (see V.A.T. Notice 742 "Land and Property"). Specialist advice on these matters should normally be sought.

## VERGES, ROADSIDE

**(See Highways—Roadside Wastes)**

## VICE-CHAIRMAN

**(See Chairman of Parish Council)**

## VILLAGE GREENS

**(See *also* Commons—Open Spaces—Recreation—
Roadside Seats and Shelters)**

In the eighteenth and nineteenth centuries, a large number of inclosures were authorised by local Inclosure Acts. In satisfaction of the rights of the inhabitants over the land inclosed, the local Act usually provided that some portion of the land should be awarded or allotted (hence the term "allotment") to the church-wardens and overseers of the parish in which it was situate, either for the benefit of the poor (e.g. as a place for cutting fuel) or as a place of recreation for the inhabitants, such as a village green or recreation ground. The general Inclosure Act of 1845 enabled a village green to be allotted to the church-wardens and overseers in trust to allow the same to be used for the purposes of exercise and recreation.

Apart from village greens allotted to the church-wardens and overseers, there are many such greens in parishes in which no inclosure was made, usually consisting of waste of the manor, on which the inhabitants of the parish have a customary right exercised for not less than 20 years to indulge in lawful sports and pastimes. Such custom constitutes land as village green and, except by failure to register under the Commons Registration Act 1965, the inhabitants cannot lawfully be deprived, by inclosure or otherwise, of their right so to use it.[1]

Village greens, in many cases, are vested in and managed by the parish council for the benefit of the inhabitants. Under the Commons Registration Act 1965, land registered as a village green where ownership was unclaimed was vested in the parish council.[2] This does not apply to greens registered after the initial registration period (1967 to 1970).

The parish council may ask the district council to make by-laws for the regulation of any village green which is for the time being under their control, or to the expense of which they have contributed. The by-laws cannot take effect until they have been confirmed by the Secretary of State. (*See* "By-laws".)

A parish council may purchase or take on lease, lay out, plant, improve and maintain lands for the purpose of being

---

[1]   *New Windsor Corporation v. Mellor* [1975] 3 All E.R. 44.
[2]   Commons Registration Act 1965, s. 8.

used as village greens, and may support or contribute to the support of land available for public use provided by any person whomsoever.[1]

A parish council must not allow a village green which it owns to be encroached upon or to be misused. If the problem is keeping vehicles off, this can usually best be achieved by digging a ditch or putting large white stones on the boundary or fencing the green (provided there is reasonable access for pedestrians). If the ownership of the green is not vested in the parish council, it will be necessary first to obtain the owner's consent. Land which is registered as village green cannot be used for car parking or caravan parking, even if the council wishes, because it is unlawful for the land not to be kept freely available for the inhabitants of the parish for lawful sports and pastimes.

The parish council, with the usual consents, may borrow money to purchase land for the purpose of being used as a village green. (*See* "Loans to Parish Councils".) The land could be acquired compulsorily. (*See* "Compulsory Purchase of Land".)

Encroachment on a village green with a defined boundary is a public nuisance and can be dealt with as such by the magistrates on the information of the parish council. Any person who wilfully injures a village green or interferes with its use as a place of recreation can be prosecuted and, if found guilty, fined up to level 1 on the standard scale for summary offences (currently £200.) He may also be required to pay for the damage caused.[2] This may be a useful weapon against persons unlawfully parking on greens.

---

[1]  P.H.A. 1875, s. 164, and L.G.A. 1972, Sch. 14, para. 27.
[2]  Inclosure Act 1857, s. 12; Commons Act 1876, s. 29.

# VILLAGE HALLS

There is a wide power available to a parish council to provide and equip suitable buildings as village halls or centres for clubs, societies or organisations having athletic, social or educational objects.[1] The council may manage such buildings with or without charge for their use or for admission, or may let them, or any portion, at a nominal or other rent to any person, club, society or organisation for use for any of the aforesaid purposes. (*See* "Recreation".) It is usual for a representative organisation, a "Community Association", to undertake the management of the building.

A parish council may also contribute to the expenses of providing or maintaining a community centre incurred by another local authority (e.g. the district or unitary council, who may provide a centre for a new housing estate in the parish under the Housing Act 1985[2]) or by a voluntary organisation, such as a Community Association. The parish council may act as trustee for a community centre provided by a voluntary organisation. Where the parish council acts as trustee for a community centre (but not where they provide one themselves as a local authority), it may be possible to claim rate relief as a charity (*see* "Rating and Valuation").

A parish council may be able to obtain a grant from the county, unitary or district council or through A.C.R.E. (*see* "Grants"). It may be possible to raise part of the cost from voluntary sources. In some areas, voluntary labour has been used. Capital expenditure falling on the parish council may be raised by borrowing (see "Loans to Parish Council").

---

[1]   L.G.(M.P.)A. 1976, s. 19.
[2]   Housing Act 1985, s. 12.

# VOTING

## (See Election and Appointment of Parish Councillors—Meetings of Parish Council)

# WARDS

## (*See also* Alteration of Areas—Parish Meeting)

Where a parish has a relatively large population, or where the population is scattered over a wide area, making it difficult to find a convenient place for a meeting of all the local government electors, or where one parish contains two or more sections with separate interests, e.g. a parish which comprises a section with a population distinctly agricultural in its pursuits and another area with a manufacturing or seafaring population, it may be convenient to divide the parish into wards for the purpose of electing councillors. In England, the procedure is governed by Part 4 of the Local Government and Public Involvement in Health Act 2007, which empowers a district, unitary or London borough council to carry out a community governance review (*see* "Alteration of Areas").

In Wales, the procedure is governed by section 57 of the Local Government Act 1972, which places a duty on county and county borough councils to keep under review the electoral arrangements for communities in their area. On a request by a community council, or at least 30 electors in a community, the Local Government Boundary Commission for Wales may review the electoral arrangements for the community, including whether or not the community should be divided into wards.

The wards will have such boundaries and such number of councillors for each ward as may be prescribed by the order made by the district or unitary council.

213

Where a parish is divided into wards, the parish councillors for each ward are elected in the same manner as councillors are elected for a parish. The rules relating to the election of councillors apply to each ward as if it were a parish. The parish councillors for all the wards will form only one parish council, and there will still be a parish meeting for the whole parish for purposes other than the election of councillors. A casual vacancy among parish councillors is filled by the whole parish council.

Where a parish is divided into wards, no local government elector may sign a nomination paper for, or vote in, more than one ward in connection with the election of councillors. There is a separate part of the register of the local government electors for each ward of a parish.

## WAR MEMORIALS

Generally, a parish council may accept, hold and administer gifts of property, real or personal, for the benefit of the inhabitants of the parish, or some part of it, and may execute any works (including works of maintenance or improvement) incidental to or consequential thereto.[1] This power may be drawn upon, for example, to enable a parish council to have transferred to it a war memorial originally purchased by voluntary subscriptions.

Another statutory power enables a parish council to incur expenditure in the maintenance, repair and protection of any war memorial within the parish, whether it is vested in the council or not.[2] A council may thus fence the memorial and repair the fence when necessary. This power was amended in 1948 to enable a parish council also to

---

[1] L.G.A. 1972, s. 139(1).
[2] War Memorials (Local Authorities' Powers) Act 1923, ss. 1 and 3.

incur expenditure in the alteration of any such memorial so as to make it serve as a memorial in connection with any war subsequent to that in connection with which it was erected, or to have corrected any error or omission in the inscription on any such memorial.[1]

## WASTE LAND AND WASTES
### (See Roadside Wastes—Untidy Land—Village Greens)

## WATERCOURSES
### (See Ditches and Drains—Nuisances and Pollution)

## WATER SUPPLY
### (See *also* Ditches and Drains)

A parish council may utilise any well, spring or stream within its parish and provide facilities for obtaining water therefrom, and may execute any works, including works of maintenance or improvement, incidental to, or consequent on, any exercise of this power.[2] The power does not authorise it to interfere with the rights of any person; nor does it restrict, in the case of a public well or other works, any powers of the district or unitary council with reference to public pumps, wells, cisterns, reservoirs, conduits and other works used for the gratuitous supply of water to the inhabitants of any part of the district, all of which vest in the district council.[3]

A parish council may contribute towards the expenses

---

[1] L.G.A. 1948, s. 133.
[2] P.H.A. 1936, s. 125.
[3] P.H.A. 1936, s. 124.

incurred by any other parish council, or by any other person, in doing anything authorised by the provision above summarised.

Thus, a parish council has very limited powers of providing a water supply for its parish. It has no authority to incur any expense in bringing water from outside the parish. A parish council is not empowered to carry out any works of magnitude involving the laying of mains, the construction of reservoirs, etc. These powers are within the province of the water undertaker, which also has the requisite powers for breaking up streets, charging water rates, etc.

Where access to a public well by the inhabitants of a parish is prevented, the parish council cannot take proceedings for the purpose of restraining interference with the access of the public to the well, as the well is vested in and under the control of the district or unitary council and it would be for that council to take action to recover damages for interference with the access of the public to the well, or for an injunction to restrain such interference. Where, however, damage is done to a well, e.g. by removing or injuring the cover to a well provided by the parish council, the parish council could bring an action for damages against the person who removed or injured the cover.

# WELL-BEING

## (See Promotion of Well-Being)

# MODEL CODE OF CONDUCT FOR COUNCILLORS IN ENGLAND[1]

## Part I
### GENERAL PROVISIONS

**Introduction and interpretation**

**1.**—(1) This Code applies to <u>you</u> as a member of an authority.

(2) You should read this Code together with the general principles prescribed by the Secretary of State.

(3) It is your responsibility to comply with the provisions of this Code.

(4) In this Code—

"meeting" means any meeting of—

(a) the authority;

(b) the executive of the authority;

(c) any of the authority's or its executive's committees, sub-committees, joint committees, joint sub-committees, or area committees;

"member" includes a co-opted member and an appointed member.

(5) In relation to a parish council, references to an authority's monitoring officer and an authority's standards committee shall be read, respectively, as references to the monitoring officer and the standards committee of the district council or unitary county council which has functions in relation to the parish council for which it is responsible under section 55(12) of the Local Government Act 2000.

---

[1] See Local Authorities (Model Code of Conduct) Order 2007 (S.I. 1159).

## Scope

**2.**—(1) Subject to sub-paragraphs (2) to (5), you must comply with this Code whenever you—

(a) conduct the business of your authority (which, in this Code, includes the business of the office to which you are elected or appointed); or

(b) act, claim to act or give the impression you are acting as a representative of your authority,

and references to your official capacity are construed accordingly.

(2) Subject to sub-paragraphs (3) and (4), this Code does not have effect in relation to your conduct other than where it is in your official capacity.

(3) In addition to having effect in relation to conduct in your official capacity, paragraphs 3(2)(c), 5 and 6(a) also have effect, at any other time, where that conduct constitutes a criminal offence for which you have been convicted.

(4) Conduct to which this Code applies (whether that is conduct in your official capacity or conduct mentioned in sub-paragraph (3)) includes a criminal offence for which you are convicted (including an offence you committed before the date you took office, but for which you are convicted after that date).

(5) Where you act as a representative of your authority—

(a) on another relevant authority, you must, when acting for that other authority, comply with that other authority's code of conduct; or

(b) on any other body, you must, when acting for that other body, comply with your authority's code of conduct, except and insofar as it conflicts with any other lawful obligations to which that other body may be subject.

## General obligations

**3.**—(1) You must treat others with respect.

(2) You must not—

    (a) do anything which may cause your authority to breach any of the equality enactments (as defined in section 33 of the Equality Act 2006);

    (b) bully any person;

    (c) intimidate or attempt to intimidate any person who is or is likely to be—

        (i) a complainant,

        (ii) a witness, or

        (iii) involved in the administration of any investigation or proceedings,

    in relation to an allegation that a member (including yourself) has failed to comply with his or her authority's code of conduct; or

    (d) do anything which compromises or is likely to compromise the impartiality of those who work for, or on behalf of, your authority.

(3) In relation to police authorities and the Metropolitan Police Authority, for the purposes of sub-paragraph (2)(d) those who work for, or on behalf of, an authority are deemed to include a police officer.

**4.** You must not—

    (a) disclose information given to you in confidence by anyone, or information acquired by you which you believe, or ought reasonably to be aware, is of a confidential nature, except where—

        (i) you have the consent of a person authorised to give it;

        (ii) you are required by law to do so;

(iii) the disclosure is made to a third party for the purpose of obtaining professional advice provided that the third party agrees not to disclose the information to any other person; or

(iv) the disclosure is—

    (aa) reasonable and in the public interest; and

    (bb) made in good faith and in compliance with the reasonable requirements of the authority; or

(b) prevent another person from gaining access to information to which that person is entitled by law.

5. You must not conduct yourself in a manner which could reasonably be regarded as bringing your office or authority into disrepute.

6. You—

(a) must not use or attempt to use your position as a member improperly to confer on or secure for yourself or any other person, an advantage or disadvantage; and

(b) must, when using or authorising the use by others of the resources of your authority—

    (i) act in accordance with your authority's reasonable requirements;

    (ii) ensure that such resources are not used improperly for political purposes (including party political purposes); and

(c) must have regard to any applicable Local Authority Code of Publicity made under the Local Government Act 1986.

7.—(1) When reaching decisions on any matter you must have regard to any relevant advice provided to you by—

(a) your authority's chief finance officer; or

(b) your authority's monitoring officer,

where that officer is acting pursuant to his or her statutory duties.

(2) You must give reasons for all decisions in accordance with any statutory requirements and any reasonable additional requirements imposed by your authority.

## Part 2
## INTERESTS

### Personal interests

8.—(1) You have a personal interest in any business of your authority where either—

  (a) it relates to or is likely to affect—

    (i) any body of which you are a member or in a position of general control or management and to which you are appointed or nominated by your authority;

    (ii) any body—

      (aa) exercising functions of a public nature;

      (bb) directed to charitable purposes; or

      (cc) one of whose principal purposes includes the influence of public opinion or policy (including any political party or trade union),

    of which you are a member or in a position of general control or management;

    (iii) any employment or business carried on by you;

    (iv) any person or body who employs or has appointed you;

    (v) any person or body, other than a relevant authority, who has made a payment to you in respect of your election or any expenses incurred by you in carrying out your duties;

    (vi) any person or body who has a place of business or land in your authority's area, and in whom you have

221

a beneficial interest in a class of securities of that person or body that exceeds the nominal value of £25,000 or one hundredth of the total issued share capital (whichever is the lower);

(vii) any contract for goods, services or works made between your authority and you or a firm in which you are a partner, a company of which you are a remunerated director, or a person or body of the description specified in paragraph (vi);

(viii) the interests of any person from whom you have received a gift or hospitality with an estimated value of at least £25;

(ix) any land in your authority's area in which you have a beneficial interest;

(x) any land where the landlord is your authority and you are, or a firm in which you are a partner, a company of which you are a remunerated director, or a person or body of the description specified in paragraph (vi) is, the tenant;

(xi) any land in the authority's area for which you have a licence (alone or jointly with others) to occupy for 28 days or longer; or

(b) a decision in relation to that business might reasonably be regarded as affecting your well-being or financial position or the well-being or financial position of a relevant person to a greater extent than the majority of—

(i) (in the case of authorities with electoral divisions or wards) other council tax payers, ratepayers or inhabitants of the electoral division or ward, as the case may be, affected by the decision;

(ii) (in the case of the Greater London Authority) other council tax payers, ratepayers or inhabitants of the Assembly constituency affected by the decision; or

      (iii) (in all other cases) other council tax payers, ratepayers or inhabitants of your authority's area.

(2) In sub-paragraph (1)(b), a relevant person is—

  (a) a member of your family or any person with whom you have a close association; or

  (b) any person or body who employs or has appointed such persons, any firm in which they are a partner, or any company of which they are directors;

  (c) any person or body in whom such persons have a beneficial interest in a class of securities exceeding the nominal value of £25,000; or

  (d) any body of a type described in sub-paragraph (1)(a)(i) or (ii).

## Disclosure of personal interests

**9.**—(1) Subject to sub-paragraphs (2) to (7), where you have a personal interest in any business of your authority and you attend a meeting of your authority at which the business is considered, you must disclose to that meeting the existence and nature of that interest at the commencement of that consideration, or when the interest becomes apparent.

(2) Where you have a personal interest in any business of your authority which relates to or is likely to affect a person described in paragraph 8(1)(a)(i) or 8(1)(a)(ii)(aa), you need only disclose to the meeting the existence and nature of that interest when you address the meeting on that business.

(3) Where you have a personal interest in any business of the authority of the type mentioned in paragraph 8(1)(a)(viii), you need not disclose the nature or existence of that interest to the meeting if the interest was registered more than three years before the date of the meeting.

(4) Sub-paragraph (1) only applies where you are aware or ought reasonably to be aware of the existence of the personal interest.

(5) Where you have a personal interest but, by virtue of paragraph 14, sensitive information relating to it is not registered in your authority's register of members' interests, you must indicate to the meeting that you have a personal interest, but need not disclose the sensitive information to the meeting.

(6) Subject to paragraph 12(1)(b), where you have a personal interest in any business of your authority and you have made an executive decision in relation to that business, you must ensure that any written statement of that decision records the existence and nature of that interest.

(7) In this paragraph, "executive decision" is to be construed in accordance with any regulations made by the Secretary of State under section 22 of the Local Government Act 2000.

**Prejudicial interest generally**

10.—(1) Subject to sub-paragraph (2), where you have a personal interest in any business of your authority you also have a prejudicial interest in that business where the interest is one which a member of the public with knowledge of the relevant facts would reasonably regard as so significant that it is likely to prejudice your judgement of the public interest.

(2) You do not have a prejudicial interest in any business of the authority where that business—

   (a) does not affect your financial position or the financial position of a person or body described in paragraph 8;

   (b) does not relate to the determining of any approval, consent, licence, permission or registration in relation to you or any person or body described in paragraph 8; or

   (c) relates to the functions of your authority in respect of—

       (i) housing, where you are a tenant of your authority provided that those functions do not relate particularly to your tenancy or lease;

    (ii) school meals or school transport and travelling expenses, where you are a parent or guardian of a child in full time education, or are a parent governor of a school, unless it relates particularly to the school which the child attends;

    (iii) statutory sick pay under Part XI of the Social Security Contributions and Benefits Act 1992, where you are in receipt of, or are entitled to the receipt of, such pay;

    (iv) an allowance, payment or indemnity given to members;

    (v) any ceremonial honour given to members; and

    (vi) setting council tax or a precept under the Local Government Finance Act 1992.

## Prejudicial interests arising in relation to overview and scrutiny committees

**11.** You also have a prejudicial interest in any business before an overview and scrutiny committee of your authority (or of a sub-committee of such a committee) where—

(a) that business relates to a decision made (whether implemented or not) or action taken by your authority's executive or another of your authority's committees, sub-committees, joint committees or joint sub-committees; and

(b) at the time the decision was made or action was taken, you were a member of the executive, committee, sub-committee, joint committee or joint sub-committee mentioned in paragraph (a) and you were present when that decision was made or action was taken.

## Effect of prejudicial interests on participation

**12.**—(1) Subject to sub-paragraph (2), where you have a prejudicial interest in any business of your authority—

(a) you must withdraw from the room or chamber where a meeting considering the business is being held—

(i) in a case where sub-paragraph (2) applies, immediately after making representations, answering questions or giving evidence;

(ii) in any other case, whenever it becomes apparent that the business is being considered at that meeting;

unless you have obtained a dispensation from your authority's standards committee;

(b) you must not exercise executive functions in relation to that business; and

(c) you must not seek improperly to influence a decision about that business.

(2) Where you have a prejudicial interest in any business of your authority, you may attend a meeting (including a meeting of the overview and scrutiny committee of your authority or of a sub-committee of such a committee) but only for the purpose of making representations, answering questions or giving evidence relating to the business, provided that the public are also allowed to attend the meeting for the same purpose, whether under a statutory right or otherwise.

## Part 3
## REGISTRATION OF MEMBERS' INTERESTS

### Registration of members' interests

13.—(1) Subject to paragraph 14, you must, within 28 days of—

(a) this Code being adopted by or applied to your authority; or

(b) your election or appointment to office (where that is later),

register in your authority's register of members' interests (maintained under section 81(1) of the Local Government Act 2000) details of your personal interests where they fall within a category mentioned in paragraph 8(1)(a), by providing written notification to your authority's monitoring officer.

(2) Subject to paragraph 14, you must, within 28 days of becoming aware of any new personal interest or change to any personal interest registered under paragraph (1), register details of that new personal interest or change by providing written notification to your authority's monitoring officer.

**Sensitive information**

**14.**—(1) Where you consider that the information relating to any of your personal interests is sensitive information, and your authority's monitoring officer agrees, you need not include that information when registering that interest, or, as the case may be, a change to that interest under paragraph 13.

(2) You must, within 28 days of becoming aware of any change of circumstances which means that information excluded under paragraph (1) is no longer sensitive information, notify your authority's monitoring officer asking that the information be included in your authority's register of members' interests.

(3) In this Code, "sensitive information" means information whose availability for inspection by the public creates, or is likely to create, a serious risk that you or a person who lives with you may be subjected to violence or intimidation.

# MODEL CODE OF CONDUCT FOR COUNCILLORS IN WALES[1]

## Part 1
### INTERPRETATION

**1.**—(1) In this code—

"co-opted member" ("*aelod cyfetholedig*"), in relation to a relevant authority, means a person who is not a member of the authority but who—

(a) is a member of any committee or sub-committee of the authority, or

(b) is a member of, and represents the authority on, any joint committee or joint sub-committee of the authority,

and who is entitled to vote on any question which falls to be decided at any meeting of that committee or sub-committee;

"meeting" ("*cyfarfod*") means any meeting—

(a) of the relevant authority,

(b) of any executive or board of the relevant authority,

(c) of any committee, sub-committee, joint committee or joint sub-committee of the relevant authority or of any such committee, sub-committee, joint committee or joint sub-committee of any executive or board of the authority, or

(d) where members or officers of the relevant authority are present other than a meeting of a political group constituted in accordance with regulation 8 of the Local Government (Committees and Political Groups) Regulations 1990,

---

[1] See Local Authorities (Model Code of Conduct) (Wales) Order 2008 (S.I. 788).

and includes circumstances in which a member of an executive or board or an officer acting alone exercises a function of an authority;

"member" ("*aelod*") includes, unless the context requires otherwise, a co-opted member;

"relevant authority" ("*awdurdod perthnasol*") means—

(a) a county council,

(b) a county borough council,

(c) a community council,

(d) a fire and rescue authority constituted by a scheme under section 2 of the Fire and Rescue Services Act 2004 or a scheme to which section 4 of that Act applies,

(e) a National Park authority established under section 63 of the Environment Act 1995;

"you" ("*chi*") means you as a member or co-opted member of a relevant authority; and

"your authority" ("*eich awdurdod*") means the relevant authority of which you are a member or co-opted member.

(2) In relation to a community council, references to an authority's monitoring officer and an authority's standards committee are to be read, respectively, as references to the monitoring officer and the standards committee of the county or county borough council which has functions in relation to the community council for which it is responsible under section 56(2) of the Local Government Act 2000.

## Part 2
## GENERAL PROVISIONS

**2.**—(1) Save where paragraph 3(a) applies, you must observe this code of conduct—

(a) whenever you conduct the business, or are present at a meeting, of your authority;

229

(b) whenever you act, claim to act or give the impression you are acting in the role of member to which you were elected or appointed;

(c) whenever you act, claim to act or give the impression you are acting as a representative of your authority; or

(d) at all times and in any capacity, in respect of conduct identified in paragraphs 6(1)(a) and 7.

(2) You should read this code together with the general principles prescribed under section 49(2) of the Local Government Act 2000 in relation to Wales.

3. Where you are elected, appointed or nominated by your authority to serve—

(a) on another relevant authority, or any other body, which includes a police authority or Local Health Board you must, when acting for that other authority or body, comply with the code of conduct of that other authority or body; or

(b) on any other body which does not have a code relating to the conduct of its members, you must, when acting for that other body, comply with this code of conduct, except and insofar as it conflicts with any other lawful obligations to which that other body may be subject.

4. You must—

(a) carry out your duties and responsibilities with due regard to the principle that there should be equality of opportunity for all people, regardless of their gender, race, disability, sexual orientation, age or religion;

(b) show respect and consideration for others;

(c) not use bullying behaviour or harass any person; and

(d) not do anything which compromises, or which is likely to compromise, the impartiality of those who work for, or on behalf of, your authority.

5.  You must not—

    (a) disclose confidential information or information which should reasonably be regarded as being of a confidential nature, without the express consent of a person authorised to give such consent, or unless required by law to do so;

    (b) prevent any person from gaining access to information to which that person is entitled by law.

6.—(1) You must—

    (a) not conduct yourself in a manner which could reasonably be regarded as bringing your office or authority into disrepute;

    (b) report, whether through your authority's confidential reporting procedure or direct to the proper authority, any conduct by another member or anyone who works for, or on behalf of, your authority which you reasonably believe involves or is likely to involve criminal behaviour (which for the purposes of this paragraph does not include offences or behaviour capable of punishment by way of a fixed penalty);

    (c) report to the Public Services Ombudsman for Wales and to your authority's monitoring officer any conduct by another member which you reasonably believe breaches this code of conduct;

    (d) not make vexatious, malicious or frivolous complaints against other members or anyone who works for, or on behalf of, your authority.

(2) You must comply with any request of your authority's monitoring officer, or the Public Services Ombudsman for Wales, in connection with an investigation conducted in accordance with their respective statutory powers.

7.  You must not—

    (a) in your official capacity or otherwise, use or attempt to use your position improperly to confer on or secure for yourself, or any other person, an advantage or create or avoid for yourself, or any other person, a disadvantage;

(b) use, or authorise others to use, the resources of your authority—

(i) imprudently;

(ii) in breach of your authority's requirements;

(iii) unlawfully;

(iv) other than in a manner which is calculated to facilitate, or to be conducive to, the discharge of the functions of the authority or of the office to which you have been elected or appointed;

(v) improperly for political purposes; or

(vi) improperly for private purposes.

8. You must—

(a) when participating in meetings or reaching decisions regarding the business of your authority, do so on the basis of the merits of the circumstances involved and in the public interest having regard to any relevant advice provided by your authority's officers, in particular by—

(i) the authority's head of paid service;

(ii) the authority's chief finance officer;

(iii) the authority's monitoring officer;

(iv) the authority's chief legal officer (who should be consulted when there is any doubt as to the authority's power to act, as to whether the action proposed lies within the policy framework agreed by the authority or where the legal consequences of action or failure to act by the authority might have important repercussions);

(b) give reasons for all decisions in accordance with any

statutory requirements and any reasonable additional requirements imposed by your authority.

**9.** You must—

   (a) observe the law and your authority's rules governing the claiming of expenses and allowances in connection with your duties as a member;

   (b) avoid accepting from anyone gifts, hospitality (other than official hospitality, such as a civic reception or a working lunch duly authorised by your authority), material benefits or services for yourself or any person which might place you, or reasonably appear to place you, under an improper obligation.

## Part 3
## INTERESTS

### Personal interests

**10.**—(1) You must in all matters consider whether you have a personal interest, and whether this code of conduct requires you to disclose that interest.

(2) You must regard yourself as having a personal interest in any business of your authority if—

   (a) it relates to, or is likely to affect—

      (i) any employment or business carried on by you;

      (ii) any person who employs or has appointed you, any firm in which you are a partner or any company for which you are a remunerated director;

      (iii) any person, other than your authority, who has made a payment to you in respect of your election or any expenses incurred by you in carrying out your duties as a member;

      (iv) any corporate body which has a place of business or land in your authority's area, and in which you have

233

a beneficial interest in a class of securities of that body that exceeds the nominal value of £25,000 or one hundredth of the total issued share capital of that body;

(v) any contract for goods, services or works made between your authority and you or a firm in which you are a partner, a company of which you are a remunerated director, or a body of the description specified in sub-paragraph (iv) above;

(vi) any land in which you have a beneficial interest and which is in the area of your authority;

(vii) any land where the landlord is your authority and the tenant is a firm in which you are a partner, a company of which you are a remunerated director, or a body of the description specified in sub-paragraph (iv) above;

(viii) any body to which you have been elected, appointed or nominated by your authority;

(ix) any—

(aa) public authority or body exercising functions of a public nature;

(bb) company, industrial and provident society, charity, or body directed to charitable purposes;

(cc) body whose principal purposes include the influence of public opinion or policy;

(dd) trade union or professional association; or

(ee) private club, society or association operating within your authority's area,

in which you have membership or hold a position of general control or management;

(x) any land in your authority's area in which you have

> a licence (alone or jointly with others) to occupy for 28 days or longer;

(b) a member of the public might reasonably perceive a conflict between your role in taking a decision, upon that business, on behalf of your authority as a whole and your role in representing the interests of constituents in your ward or electoral division; or

(c) a decision upon it might reasonably be regarded as affecting—

   (i) your well-being or financial position, or that of a person with whom you live, or any person with whom you have a close personal association;

   (ii) any employment or business carried on by persons as described in 10(2)(c)(i);

   (iii) any person who employs or has appointed such persons described in 10(2)(c)(i), any firm in which they are a partner, or any company of which they are directors;

   (iv) any corporate body in which persons as described in 10(2)(c)(i) have a beneficial interest in a class of securities exceeding the nominal value of £5,000; or

   (v) any body listed in paragraphs 10(2)(a)(ix)(aa) to (ee) in which persons described in 10(2)(c)(i) hold a position of general control or management,

   to a greater extent than the majority of—

      (aa) in the case of an authority with electoral divisions or wards, other council tax payers, rate payers or inhabitants of the electoral division or ward, as the case may be, affected by the decision; or

      (bb) in all other cases, other council tax payers, ratepayers or inhabitants of the authority's area.

## Disclosure of personal interests

**11.**—(1) Where you have a personal interest in any business of your authority and you attend a meeting at which that business is considered, you must disclose orally to that meeting the existence and nature of that interest before or at the commencement of that consideration, or when the interest becomes apparent.

(2) Where you have a personal interest in any business of your authority and you make—

    (a) written representations (whether by letter, facsimile or some other form of electronic communication) to a member or officer of your authority regarding that business, you should include details of that interest in the written communication; or

    (b) oral representations (whether in person or some form of electronic communication) to a member or officer of your authority you should disclose the interest at the commencement of such representations, or when it becomes apparent to you that you have such an interest, and confirm the representation and interest in writing within 14 days of the representation.

(3) Subject to paragraph 14(1)(b) below, where you have a personal interest in any business of your authority and you have made a decision in exercising a function of an executive or board, you must in relation to that business ensure that any written statement of that decision records the existence and nature of your interest.

(4) You must, in respect of a personal interest not previously disclosed, before or immediately after the close of a meeting where the disclosure is made pursuant to sub-paragraph 11(1), give written notification to your authority in accordance with any requirements identified by your authority's monitoring officer from time to time but, as a minimum containing—

    (a) details of the personal interest;

(b) details of the business to which the personal interest relates; and

(c) your signature.

(5) Where you have agreement from your monitoring officer that the information relating to your personal interest is sensitive information, pursuant to paragraph 16(1), your obligations under this paragraph 11 to disclose such information, whether orally or in writing, are to be replaced with an obligation to disclose the existence of a personal interest and to confirm that your monitoring officer has agreed that the nature of such personal interest is sensitive information.

(6) For the purposes of sub-paragraph (4), a personal interest will only be deemed to have been previously disclosed if written notification has been provided in accordance with this code since the last date on which you were elected, appointed or nominated as a member of your authority.

(7) For the purposes of sub-paragraph (3), where no written notice is provided in accordance with that paragraph you will be deemed as not to have declared a personal interest in accordance with this code.

**Prejudicial interests**

12.—(1) Subject to sub-paragraph (2) below, where you have a personal interest in any business of your authority you also have a prejudicial interest in that business if the interest is one which a member of the public with knowledge of the relevant facts would reasonably regard as so significant that it is likely to prejudice your judgement of the public interest.

(2) Subject to sub-paragraph (3), you will not be regarded as having a prejudicial interest in any business where that business—

(a) relates to—

(i) another relevant authority of which you are also a member;

(ii) another public authority or body exercising functions of a public nature in which you hold a position of general control or management;

(iii) a body to which you have been elected, appointed or nominated by your authority;

(iv) your role as a school governor (where not appointed or nominated by your authority) unless it relates particularly to the school of which you are a governor;

(v) your role as a member of a Local Health Board where you have not been appointed or nominated by your authority;

(b) relates to—

(i) the housing functions of your authority where you hold a tenancy or lease with your authority, provided that you do not have arrears of rent with your authority of more than two months, and provided that those functions do not relate particularly to your tenancy or lease;

(ii) the functions of your authority in respect of school meals, transport and travelling expenses, where you are a guardian, parent, grandparent or have parental responsibility (as defined in section 3 of the Children Act 1989) of a child in full time education, unless it relates particularly to the school which that child attends;

(iii) the functions of your authority in respect of statutory sick pay under Part XI of the Social Security Contributions and Benefits Act 1992, where you are in receipt of, or are entitled to the receipt of such pay from your authority;

(iv) the functions of your authority in respect of an allowance or payment made under sections 22(5), 24(4) and 173 to 176 of the Local Government Act

1972, an allowance or pension under section 18 of the Local Government and Housing Act 1989 or an allowance or payment under section 100 of the Local Government Act 2000;

(c) your role as a community councillor in relation to a grant, loan or other form of financial assistance made by your community council to community or voluntary organisations up to a maximum of £500.

(3) The exemptions in sub-paragraph (2)(a) do not apply where the business relates to the determination of any approval, consent, licence, permission or registration.

## Overview and scrutiny committees

**13.** You also have a prejudicial interest in any business before an overview and scrutiny committee of your authority (or of a sub-committee of such a committee where—

(a) that business relates to a decision made (whether implemented or not) or action taken by your authority's executive, board or another of your authority's committees, sub-committees, joint committees or joint sub-committees; and

(b) at the time the decision was made or action was taken, you were a member of the executive, board, committee, sub-committee, joint-committee or joint sub-committee mentioned in sub-paragraph (a) and you were present when that decision was made or action was taken.

## Participation in relation to disclosed interests

**14.**—(1) Subject to sub-paragraphs (2), (3) and (4), where you have a prejudicial interest in any business of your authority you must, unless you have obtained a dispensation from your authority's standards committee—

(a) withdraw from the room, chamber or place where a meeting considering the business is being held—

(i) where sub-paragraph (2) applies, immediately after the period for making representations, answering questions or giving evidence relating to the business has ended and in any event before further consideration of the business begins, whether or not the public are allowed to remain in attendance for such consideration; or

(ii) in any other case, whenever it becomes apparent that that business is being considered at that meeting;

(b) not exercise executive or board functions in relation to that business;

(c) not seek to influence a decision about that business;

(d) not make any written representations (whether by letter, facsimile or some other form of electronic communication) in relation to that business; and

(e) not make any oral representations (whether in person or some form of electronic communication) in respect of that business or immediately cease to make such oral representations when the prejudicial interest becomes apparent.

(2) Where you have a prejudicial interest in any business of your authority you may attend a meeting but only for the purpose of making representations, answering questions or giving evidence relating to the business, provided that the public are also allowed to attend the meeting for the same purpose, whether under a statutory right or otherwise.

(3) Sub-paragraph (1) does not prevent you attending and participating in a meeting if—

(a) you are required to attend a meeting of an overview or scrutiny committee, by such committee exercising its statutory powers; or

(b) you have the benefit of a dispensation provided that you—

(i) state at the meeting that you are relying on the dispensation; and

(ii) before or immediately after the close of the meeting give written notification to your authority containing—

(aa) details of the prejudicial interest;

(bb) details of the business to which the prejudicial interest relates;

(cc) details of, and the date on which, the dispensation was granted; and

(dd) your signature.

(4) Where you have a prejudicial interest and are making written or oral representations to your authority in reliance upon a dispensation, you must provide details of the dispensation within any such written or oral representation and, in the latter case, provide written notification to your authority within 14 days of making the representation.

## Part 4
## THE REGISTER OF MEMBERS' INTERESTS

**Registration of financial and other interests and memberships and management positions**

15.—(1) Subject to sub-paragraph (3), you must, within 28 days of—

(a) your authority's code of conduct being adopted or the mandatory provisions of this model code being applied to your authority; or

(b) your election or appointment to office (if that is later),

register your financial interests and other interests, where they fall within a category mentioned in paragraph 10(2)(a) in your authority's register maintained under section 81(1) of the Local Government Act 2000 by providing written notification to your authority's monitoring officer.

(2) You must, within 28 days of becoming aware of any new personal interest or change to any personal interest

241

registered under sub-paragraph (1), register that new personal interest or change by providing written notification to your authority's monitoring officer.

(3) Sub-paragraphs (1) and (2) do not apply to sensitive information determined in accordance with paragraph 16(1).

(4) Sub-paragraph (1) will not apply if you are a member of a relevant authority which is a community council when you act in your capacity as a member of such an authority.

## Sensitive information

**16.**—(1) Where you consider that the information relating to any of your personal interests is sensitive information, and your authority's monitoring officer agrees, you need not include that information when registering that interest, or, as the case may be, a change to the interest under paragraph 15.

(2) You must, within 28 days of becoming aware of any change of circumstances which means that information excluded under sub-paragraph (1) is no longer sensitive information, notify your authority's monitoring officer asking that the information be included in your authority's register of members' interests.

(3) In this code, "sensitive information" ("*gwybodaeth sensitif*") means information whose availability for inspection by the public creates, or is likely to create, a serious risk that you or a person who lives with you may be subjected to violence or intimidation.

## Registration of gifts and hospitality

**17.** You must, within 28 days of receiving any gift, hospitality, material benefit or advantage above a value specified in a resolution of your authority, provide written notification to your authority's monitoring officer of the existence and nature of that gift, hospitality, material benefit or advantage.

## Appendix 3

## FORMS AND RECORDS

published by
SHAW & SONS LIMITED
for the use of
**LOCAL COUNCILS**
(Parish Councils, Town Councils
and Community Councils)

*All the documents listed on the following pages may be ordered from:*

Shaw & Sons Limited
Shaway House
21 Bourne Park
Bourne Road
Crayford
Kent DA1 4BZ

Tel: 01322 621100
Fax: 01322 550553
E-mail: sales@shaws.co.uk

*Further information about all Shaw's products and services can be found at*
**www.shaws.co.uk**

| Catalogue No. | *Description* |
|---|---|

## Accounts

**PC6**    **Receipts and payments book**
specially designed to provide the information required by the
Financial Statements (Parishes) Regulations, comprising:–
     6 pages Burial Grounds Account
     16 openings General and other Accounts
     4 pages Charities Account
     4 pages Allotments Account
     2 openings Loans and Sales of Assets Account
*page size 14" x 9"*

**PC6G**    **Receipts and payments book**
with blank column headings      *book of 50 leaves*

**PC6A**    **Annual receipts and payments book**
with blank column headings    *manilla covered book of 12 openings*
(this is particularly suitable for small parishes and will enable
accounts to continue to be kept in a new volume each year
whilst the previous year's book is with the auditors)

**PC12**    **Assets register**      *bound book of 24 openings*
*manilla covered book of 12 openings*

**PC13B**    **Parish council receipt book**      *book of 100 in duplicate*

**LD**    **General receipt book**      *book of 100 in duplicate*

**AG20**    **Allotment rent book**      *book of 100 leaves*

**AG18**    **Allotment garden rent receipt book**, two entries per leaf
*book of 50 in duplicate*

**BUR32A**    **Burial fees receipt book**      *book of 50 in duplicate*

**BUR22**    **Burial fees account book**      *book of 50 leaves*
*book of 100 leaves*

## Allotment Gardens

**AG2A**    **Application for allotment garden** (model form)

**AG6F**    **Agreement for letting** (model form) – full form

**AG4**    **Notice of determination of tenancy** under s.30 of the
1908 Act

**AG5**    **Register of allotment gardens**, with columns for
particulars of tenancy, etc.      *book of 50 leaves*

244

## Forms and records

| Catalogue No. | Description | |
|---|---|---|
| **AG20** | **Allotment rent book** | *book of 100 leaves* |
| **AG18** | **Allotment garden rent receipt book**, two entries per leaf | *book of 50 in duplicate* |

### AUDIT

**LG11**   **Notice of audit** for parish council, community council or town council

### AUTHORITIES TO ENTER

**RF9 Cert**   **Authority to enter premises** (general form)
folding card to be carried by officer, with provision for photograph

**RF9 Wall**   **Wallet for above**

**RF9 Comp**   **Authority to enter premises**, complete with wallet

### BOOKS AND DOCUMENTS

**QS1(100)**   **Register of deeds**
*book of 100 leaves, with index cut through fore-edge*

**QS1**   **Loose-leaf ledger sheets**   *pack of 100*

**QS2**   **Index to papers**   *loose-leaf sheets, $8^3/_8$" x 14"*

### BURIAL AND CREMATION

REGISTERS RELATING TO GRAVES

**BUR3A**   **Register of graves** – general pattern (6 grave spaces per page)   *book of 100 pages*
*book of 200 pages*

**BUR3B**   **Register of graves and grants of exclusive right of burial**
(8 grave spaces per page)   *book of 100 pages*
*book of 200 pages*

**BUR12**   **Register of public graves in consecrated ground**
(8 grave spaces per page)   *book of 100 pages*

**BUR13**   **Register of public graves in unconsecrated ground**
(8 grave spaces per page)   *book of 100 pages*

**BUR4**   **Register of purchased graves**
(8 grave spaces per page)   *book of 100 pages*
*book of 200 pages*
*book of 300 pages*

# Appendix 3

| Catalogue No. | Description |
|---|---|

**GRANTS OF EXCLUSIVE RIGHT OF BURIAL**

**BB24**    **Grant of exclusive right of burial**    *book of 50 in duplicate*
*book of 100 in duplicate*

*Grants can also be printed to order incorporating local particulars.*
*Please enquire for details.*

**BUR35**    **Register of grants of exclusive right of burial**
*book of 50 openings*

**BUR3B**    **Register of graves and grants of exclusive right of burial**
(8 grave spaces per page)    *book of 100 pages*
*book of 200 pages*

**BUR17**    **Assignment of exclusive right of burial**

**BUR16**    **Register of transfers of exclusive right of burial**
*book of 100 pages*

**REGISTERS RELATING TO BURIALS AND MORTUARIES**

**BUR6**    **Register of burials** (8 names per opening)
*book of 100 openings*
*book of 200 openings*

**BUR11**    **Index to register of burials**
*book of 50 leaves, with index cut through fore-edge*

**BUR10**    **Register of disinterments** (8 names per opening)
*book of 25 openings*
*book of 50 openings*

**NOTICES AND CERTIFICATES**

**BUR29**    **Notice to burial authority of intended interment**

**MISCELLANEOUS**

**BUR7**    **Certified extracts from the register of burials**
*book of 50 openings*

**BUR32A**    **Receipts for interment fees paid**    *book of 50 in duplicate*

**BUR22**    **Burial fees account book**    *book of 50 leaves*
*book of 100 leaves*

**BOOKS OF CONDOLENCE**

**IM1/50**    **In memoriam condolence book** – 10 entries per page
*book of 50 leaves*

**IM1/100**    **Ditto**    *book of 100 leaves*

| Catalogue No. | Description |
| --- | --- |
| **IM2/50** | **In memoriam condolence book** – ruled border only<br>*book of 50 leaves* |
| **IM2/100** | **Ditto** *book of 100 leaves* |
| | FORMS RELATING TO THE ERECTION OF MONUMENTS |
| **BUR36** | **Application for grant of right to erect and maintain, or add inscription to, memorial** |
| **BUR37** | **Grant of right to erect and maintain, or add inscription to, memorial**, with copy for cemetery superintendent<br>*book of 50 in duplicate* |
| **BUR34** | **Register of memorials** (8 entries per opening)<br>*book of 50 openings* |

## ELECTION OF LOCAL COUNCILLORS

| | |
| --- | --- |
| **CLG11** | **Notice of vacancy in office** of councillor |
| **PC9** | **Public notice of vacancy in office** of parish councillor |
| **TC9** | **Public notice of vacancy in office** of town councillor |
| **CC9** | **Public notice of vacancy in office** of community councillor |
| **PCE34** | **Notice to person elected** as parish or town councillor<br>*pack of 25* |
| **WE34BL** | **Notice to person elected** as community councillor (bilingual) *pack of 25* |
| **LE40** | **Declaration of acceptance of office** by chairman or councillor *pack of 25* |
| **LE40/2** | **Declaration of acceptance of office** by chairman or councillor *book of 200 entries* |
| **EW40BL** | **Declaration of acceptance of office** by chairman or councillor – bilingual Welsh/English *pack of 25* |
| **EW40/2BL** | **Ditto** *book of 200 entries* |

## EXPENSES

| | |
| --- | --- |
| **RF5** | **Log book** for officers using own cars for official purposes<br>*book of 23 openings* |
| **RF6** | **Claim for subsistence allowance and travelling expenses** |
| **IB1C** | **"Ideal" permanent cover** for log book |

| Catalogue No. | Description |
|---|---|

## INTERESTS

MODEL CODE OF CONDUCT (ENGLISH REGULATIONS)

**LGA1**    **Notification by member** of a local authority of personal
interests              *pack of 25*

**LGA3**    **Notification by member** of a local authority of change to
personal interests

**LGA10**    **Record of members' interests**
*loose-leaf sheets, 13" x 16$^1/_2$"*

**NETA(8)**    **"Neta" loose-leaf binder**, to hold above sheets

**LGA10A**    **Register of members' interests** – as above but in book
form suitable for parish councils
*manilla covered book of 50 openings*

**LGA11**    **Register of gifts or hospitality** received by members
*manilla covered book of 25 openings*

**LGA25**    **Disclosure by member** of local authority of personal
interest in a matter under consideration at a meeting

CODE OF CONDUCT (WELSH REGULATIONS)
*Please note these forms are written in English but conform to
Welsh legislation*

**LGA1W**    **Notification by member** of a local authority of personal
interests

**LGA2W**    **Notification by member** of a local authority of receipt of
gift, hospitality, benefit or advantage

**LGA3W**    **Notification by member** of a local authority of change to
personal interests

**LGA10W**    **Record of members' financial or other interests**
*loose-leaf sheets, 13" x 16$^1/_2$"*

**NETA(8)**    **"Neta" loose-leaf binder**, to hold above sheets

**LGA10AW**    **Register of members' interests** – as above but in book
form suitable for community councils
*manilla covered book of 50 openings*

**LGA11W**    **Register of gifts or hospitality** received by members
*manilla book of 25 openings*

| Catalogue No. | Description |
|---|---|

## LAND

**ML33**    **Requisition for information as to persons interested in land** (Local Government (Miscellaneous Provisions) Act 1972, s.16)

**ML33A**    **Ditto** – with tear-off reply form attached

## MEETINGS OF LOCAL COUNCIL

PARISH COUNCILS

**PC3B**    **Public notice of annual meeting** of parish council

**MC1P**    **Notice to councillor of annual meeting** of parish council

**PC4**    **Ditto** (alternative pattern)

**PC2M**    **Public notice of ordinary meeting** of parish council

**PC2**    **Notice to councillor of ordinary meeting** of parish council

**PC3**    **Ditto** (alternative pattern)

TOWN COUNCILS

**TC2**    **Public notice of annual meeting** of town council

**TC3**    **Notice to councillor of annual meeting** of town council

**TC4**    **Ditto** (alternative pattern)

**TC6**    **Public notice of ordinary meeting** of town council

**TC7**    **Notice to councillor of ordinary meeting** of town council

**TC8**    **Ditto** (alternative pattern)

COMMUNITY COUNCILS

**CC2**    **Public notice of annual meeting** of community council

**CC3**    **Notice to councillor of annual meeting** of community council

**CC4**    **Ditto** (alternative pattern)

**CC6**    **Public notice of ordinary meeting** of community council

**CC7**    **Notice to councillor of ordinary meeting** of community council

**CC8**    **Ditto** (alternative pattern)

| Catalogue No. | Description |
| --- | --- |

RECORDS OF MEETINGS

**HM20**    **Attendance register for signature by councillors**, with summary (contains both HM20 and HM21)    *book of 50 leaves*

**HM21**    **Attendance register** (date of meetings only), with columns for recording attendances
*book of 50 leaves*

**HM22**    **Motion book** for entering notices of motions to be made at meetings    *book of 50 leaves*

**PC1**    **Minute book**, with rules as to meetings and proceedings of parish meetings, parish councils and committees printed in front, numbered and indexed    *book of 150 leaves*

**CC1**    **Minute book**, with rules as to meetings and proceedings of community meetings, community councils and committees printed in front, numbered and indexed    *book of 150 leaves*

**MINA4**    **Minute book** – a four-post semi-lockable binder which takes standard A4 punched paper    *different colours available*

**MINA4GB** **Minute guard book** – an oversized A4 casebound book with guard slips in the spine, allowing minutes to be pasted into it without bulking    *book of 100 leaves*

PARISH, TOWN OR COMMUNITY MEETINGS

**PM2**    **Public notice of annual parish meeting**

**PM3**    **Public notice of ordinary parish meeting**

**TM2**    **Public notice of annual town meeting**

**TM3**    **Public notice of ordinary town meeting**

**CM3**    **Public notice of community meeting**

## POLITICAL GROUPS

THE LOCAL GOVERNMENT (COMMITTEES AND POLITICAL GROUPS) REGULATIONS 1990

**CLG30**    **Notice of constitution** of a political group

**CLG30W** **Hysbysiad o sefydlu grwp gwleidyddol** (Welsh language version)

**CLG31**    **Notice of change of name** of [group] [leader] [deputy leader]

| Catalogue No. | Description |
|---|---|

**CLG31W** **Hysbysiad o newid enw** [grwp gwleidyddol] [arweinydd] [cynrychiolydd] (Welsh language version)

**CLG32** **Notice by member** of wish to join a political group [and request for review of arrangements for allocation of seats]

**CLG32W** **Hysbysiad o ddymuniad i ymuno** â grwp gwleidyddol [a chais am adolygiad o'r trefniadau] (Welsh language version)

**CLG33** **Notice by member** of wish no longer to be treated as a member of a political group

**CLG33W** **Hysbysiad o ddymuniad i beidio** bod mwyach yn aelod o grwp gwleidyddol (Welsh language version)

**CLG34** **Notice by members** of a political group of wish for a member no longer to be treated as a member of that group

**CLG34W** **Hysbysiad o ddymuniad i aelod beidio** a chael ei ystyried mwyach yn aelod o grwp gwleidyddol (Welsh language version)

**CLG35** **Notice by proper officer** of [allocation] [vacation] of seat(s) on body(ies)

**CLG35W** **Hysbysiad o** [neilltuo] [gwacáu] sedd(au) (Welsh language version)

## PRECEPTS

**PC5** **Precept by parish council upon principal authority**
*single form*

**TC5** **Precept by town council upon principal authority**
*single form*

**CC5** **Precept by community council upon principal authority**
*single form*

## PROPERTY OF LOCAL COUNCIL

**DC63** **Record of properties** belonging to the council
(sold in multiples of 25)  *loose-leaf sheets, 13" x 11¹/₄"*

## RECREATION FACILITIES

**A16H** **Council room or hall lettings book**  *book of 25 leaves*
*book of 50 leaves*

251

## Appendix 3